10269293

D0299174

PRESERVE OR DESTROY

Tourism and the Environment

Jonathan Croall spent several years in book publishing – with Cassell, Penguin, Oxford University Press, and Writers and Readers – before turning to writing and journalism. He is the author of *Neill of Summerhill: The Permanent Rebel, Don't You Know There's a War On?: The People's Voice 1939-1945, Don't Shoot the Goalkeeper, Dig for History*, the Gulbenkian Foundation's *Helping to Heal: The Arts in Health Care* (with Peter Senior), and a children's novel, *Sent Away*. He is a former features editor of the *Times Educational Supplement*, and editor and co-founder of *Arts Express* magazine. Now freelance, he edits the National Theatre magazine *StageWrite*, and writes for the *Guardian, Observer, Times Educational Supplement* and other national newspapers on education, environment and arts topics.

Front cover photograph: *Dovedale in the Peak District (Peak District National Park)*

PRESERVE OR DESTROY

Tourism and the Environment

Jonathan Croall

Calouste Gulbenkian Foundation, London

For Nicki, my fellow-traveller, with much love

Published by Calouste Gulbenkian Foundation
98 Portland Place
London
W1N 4ET
Tel: 0171 636 5313

© Calouste Gulbenkian Foundation
First Published 1995
Reprinted 1997

The right of Jonathan Croall to be identified as the author of this work has been asserted by him in accordance with the Copyright, Designs and Patents Act 1988.

British Library Cataloguing-in-Publication Data
A catalogue record for this book is available from the British Library

ISBN 0 - 903319 - 69 - 1

Designed by Maddison/Moore Associates
Printed and bound in the UK by Marstan Press

Contents

Acknowledgements

Many people in Britain and the Republic of Ireland – in tourist boards, academic institutions, government departments, environmental organisations and elsewhere – have helped me to put this book together. They have done so either by talking to me, supplying me with documents, or putting me in touch with projects and individuals concerned with tourism. It's a cliché to say that they're too numerous to mention, but they are. Nevertheless, I thank them all warmly for their time and invaluable assistance.

I would, however, specifically like to express my gratitude to those who gave me their time while I was compiling my four main case-studies: Chris Lewis from the Peak District Partnership, Beverley Trowbridge from the Tarka Project in Devon, Alison Turnock from the Purbeck Heritage Committee in Dorset, and Barry Collins from Center Parcs in Nottinghamshire.

At the Calouste Gulbenkian Foundation I must thank Ben Whitaker, for commissioning the book and offering helpful comments on my initial draft; Denny Robson, for her valuable editorial support; and Millicent Bowerman and Lynne Cope for their patient assistance during the book's writing and production. Finally, thanks to John Maddison for bringing his design skills to the book.

Picture Credits

British Trust for Conservation Volunteers: page 76
Devon County Council: page 51
Andrew Hallam: page 131
Robert Harding Picture Library: pages 6, 23, 59, 85, 105, 143
Heart of England Tourist Board: page 116
Images: pages 16, 94
Lake District National Park: page 151
National Trust: page 34
Northern Ireland Tourist Board: page 123
Peak Tourism Partnership: page 42
Punch: page 4

Foreword
by Jonathon Porritt

The travel and tourism industry is in the frontline debate about sustainable development. How can the industry continue to prosper without damaging either the local environments or the local cultures on which it depends? Happily, Jonathan Croall spares us the usual tedious terminological treatise about what sustainability does or does not mean. In reality, we all know what it means, and we all know that it's more or less insane to be leading our lives and creating wealth in ways that are obviously unsustainable.

Travel and tourism simply have to get it right. Not because the quality of life of people like you and I owes so much to the benefits of travel, but because the prospects of millions of people in the third world depend absolutely on the industry getting it right.

Right now, of course, the industry is still mostly getting it wrong. *Preserve or Destroy* confronts the scale of the environmental, social and cultural damage head on, from the utterly horrific harm which is being done through the phenomenon of sex tourism, through to the rather more subtle effects of ever-popular corners of our world being 'loved to death' – even by those who care the most about them. With more than one billion leisure visits to the UK countryside already taking place every year, just how much potential is there for any genuinely sustainable growth?

No one any longer disputes the scale of the problems caused by those negative impacts. But how best should we respond? By cutting off funds to precisely those bodies (such as the English Tourist Board) that could help to put tourism on to a more sustainable footing? By castigating the entire industry as an agent of dastardly environmental evil? Or by lapsing into indifference or self-inflicted powerlessness, insisting that we all have the right to switch off our environmental consciences when we're on holiday or even thinking about the next holiday?

Absolutely not!

The principal message of this timely and fascinating study is that many initiatives are already under way, and that many, many initiatives could and should be under way soon. I lost track thinking of the people and organisations that could benefit directly from picking up on the many examples of best practice outlined in this book.

Vicious circles don't become benign circles overnight or without a great deal of effort on all sides. But the blueprint for that transformation, at least in the UK, is sketched out here in a style that is both realistic and positive.

Introduction: The Spectre of Tourism

A spectre is haunting our planet: the spectre of tourism. It's said that travel broadens the mind. Today, in its modern guise of tourism, it can also ruin landscapes, destroy communities, pollute the air and water, trivialise cultures, bring about uniformity, and generally contribute to the continuing degradation of life on our planet.

Tourism on the scale we now know it is a comparatively recent phenomenon. Over the last thirty years, the growth in leisure time and the availability of cheap travel have caused a massive worldwide explosion. Millions of people are now able to travel with increasing ease and regularity beyond their own regions or frontiers, with a chance to get to know new peoples and new countries.

But this change has brought some appalling consequences in its wake. The increasing demand for tourist facilities in more and more countries has, through the actions of greedy, unscrupulous or unthinking governments, developers and tour operators, resulted in many places in massively inappropriate development. The arrival of mass tourism has led to the ruin of fine coastlines, the deforestation of alpine areas, the erosion of precious rural landscapes, and the destruction of unique wilderness areas and wildlife habitats. Erstwhile quiet beauty spots have become 'honeypots', many of them being gradually eroded by the tramping feet of hundreds of thousands of visitors. Meanwhile overcrowding in many areas has led to growing congestion on the roads, resulting in increased levels of noise and pollution. Some of the best-loved places in the global landscape are being gradually 'loved to death'.

But the widespread damage has not been confined to the physical environment. In many countries it has also had an adverse effect on the traditional ways of life, and on the distinctiveness of local cultures. Many people have been uprooted from their communities, their traditional skills lost to the area simply because it has suddenly been developed for the benefit of the tourist trade. Yet all too often such developments have been imposed from outside, without any effort to involve people in decisions that have such a profound effect on their lives and livelihoods.

Tourism is the world's fastest growing industry. By the year 2000 it will, according to most estimates, be the largest. By some accounts it has already achieved this status. Yet already, in areas as diverse as the Mediterranean, the Alps, the English Lake District, and the mountains of Nepal, the situation has reached crisis point. The predicted increase in the number of visitors coming to these and other areas between now and the millennium makes awesome reading, and suggests that the consequences could be devastating unless radical changes are made in policies, behaviour and attitudes.

What can be done to halt and perhaps even reverse the damage created by so much tourist activity, before it becomes too late to take effective action? Fortunately, there is now a slowly spreading belief that this deteriorating situation should not be allowed to continue unchecked. Some of the more enlightened people within the tourism industry are at last beginning to realise they are slowly killing off the very resource on which their livelihoods depend. Meanwhile an increasing environmental awareness in many countries is leading to a growing understanding of the need to develop alternative approaches, to try to encourage and promote a different kind of tourism that both recognises the fragility of the natural environment, and respects the needs and aspirations of the people that live in the areas affected.

This new kind of tourism, which is generally seen as being at the opposite end of the spectrum to mass tourism, has been given many labels. Among the most common are 'green tourism', 'responsible tourism', 'alternative tourism', 'ecotourism' and 'sustainable tourism'. However, these terms are by no means interchangeable, although they are sometimes used as if they were. They tend to be used loosely, even misleadingly – for example by tour operators and tourist organisations, as a way of marketing their products or flaunting their environmentally responsible credentials. Yet the different meanings of these terms are important, and need to be looked at in some detail. In this book I concentrate on the notion of sustainable tourism, which seems to me the term that provides the most useful perspective. It's a concept that puts tourism into the mainstream of the general economic, social and moral debate about sustainable development, and one that is gradually creeping into the language – even if there is by no means a consensus as to what it actually means in practice.

As the negative side of tourism has become more evident, as well as increasingly well-publicised, many of those working in or concerned with tourism – academics, planning officers, environmental activists, local and national politicians, small businesses, even some tour operators – have come to recognise the need for action to try to ameliorate the situation. In the UK and elsewhere, there are now many projects and initiatives up and running in which solutions are being sought to such problems, and efforts being made to encourage a more sustainable approach. An increasing number of conferences and seminars is being held in different countries, most of them dedicated to discussing how tourism can be made more sustainable. But mere talk is not enough, as many people have recognised. Attempts are being made to persuade tourism businesses large and small that a sustainable approach is not only morally desirable and environmentally wise, but also good for business in the long run. It is, however, an uphill battle.

Tourism of course embraces many kinds of activity, undertaken for a whole range of reasons. For the purposes of this book I define a tourist as someone who makes a journey for leisure purposes to a place more than ten miles from their own home. This embraces annual holidays taken at home or abroad, weekend breaks, day trips, leisure time during business travel, adventure and activity holidays, special interest holidays, and other kinds. It takes people to a huge variety of rural, coastal, mountain and wilderness destinations, many of which until recently have been free from an influx of outsiders. These are the areas on which I have chosen to concentrate. I have generally not dealt with the similar but different problems caused by tourism in large towns and cities, since these raise other issues which would need more space for discussion than I have available.

Not long ago mass tourism was effectively confined to the developed countries. Even as recently as 1992, some 80% of all international travel was undertaken by people from just twenty countries. That picture is now changing rapidly and tourism is fast becoming a global phenomenon. So, while the focus of this book is the United Kingdom and the Republic of Ireland, and all my case-studies are taken from these countries, I have briefly touched on problems and initiatives in other parts of the world that are relevant to any examination of sustainable tourism.

In some of these areas, especially in Europe, the most urgent question is how the damage inflicted by tourism can be stopped, and what we can do to repair it in the short or medium term. Elsewhere, especially but not exclusively in the developing world, the need is to decide how the mistakes made by other countries in the last thirty years can be avoided. Such questions will not have any easy answers.

"......Now, at Starfish Bay, you're miles away from anyone ——

that's what everyone likes about it."

MAJORITY REPORT

1 The Scale of the Problem

'I beg you, please don't come to Hawaii. Tourism is killing us, it is literally sucking the life out of us.'

Puhipau, Hawaiian activist[1]

Tourism and travel are about change, adventure, relaxation, new experiences, unfamiliar landscapes. They can help to refresh our spirits, shift our perspective on our daily lives, increase our understanding of how other people live. They may also give us new insights into the culture and politics of a country or region, or help us to appreciate the distinctive character of different localities.

This is the positive side of tourism. Yet it's an activity that can also be destructive, as has become very clear in recent years. Very often the costs – environmental, social and cultural – seem to outweigh the benefits. The very places which appeal to us because of their isolation or beauty, or because they are so different from our everyday surroundings, are in danger of being spoilt, changed or becoming less distinctive, simply by dint of the sheer numbers of us who want to visit them. Tourism at its worst has caused overcrowding, damage to the physical environment, conflicts within communities, increases in crime and prostitution, traffic congestion and pollution, and an incalculable amount of inappropriate development in some of the world's most beautiful regions.

This damaging process is far advanced in many places. Predictions about the increase in tourist travel suggest it will continue, even accelerate. Tourism is on course to be the world's biggest industry by the year 2000. According to some analysts, it is already at the top of the league, generating 1 in 15 jobs worldwide and 1 in 10 in the European Community. The World Tourism Organisation measures its growth by calculating 'tourist arrivals' across national boundaries. These rose from 25 million in 1950 to 500 million in 1993. In other words, nearly 8% of

Kamari Beach, Santorini, Greece. Over 100 million people visit the Mediterranean region every year.

the world's population chose to travel in that year. Over the same forty-year period the number of domestic tourists has tripled. By the turn of the century there could be 637 million travellers worldwide on the move every year. This huge growth is graphically reflected in the case of Venice which, with only 83,000 residents, now receives on average a staggering

100,000 visitors a day. Small wonder that the idea of charging tourists to enter the city has been floated more than once.

Much of this spectacular growth can be put down to the huge rise in popularity of package holidays, which began to make an impact in Britain and other countries after the Second World War. These cheap, all-in holidays have transformed the leisure lives of millions, and brought places that previously seemed accessible only to the better-off within easy reach of most people, at least in the developed countries. Of course, many of us positively enjoy taking our holidays surrounded by crowds of other people. But the cost has been great: blighted coastlines, ugly and poor-quality buildings, destruction of wildlife, pollution of the sea and beaches, loss of basic amenities by local people, and the increasing bastardisation of traditional arts and crafts.

Meanwhile in the UK tourism grows apace. The country ranks sixth in the world's most popular destinations, behind the US, France, Spain, Italy and Austria, and fifth amongst the largest national tourism industries. Recent projections suggest continuing growth for the rest of the decade, especially in the number of foreign visitors, of whom over 19 million visited in 1993. Such growth is one of the factors that has led to an increase in the number of tourist attractions: according to the English Tourist Board, this rose from 2,300 in 1983 to 3,000 in 1987 to 4,840 in 1992.

Around the world, the question of visitor numbers is becoming an increasingly urgent one, as the most popular tourist spots become seriously overloaded. The scale of the crisis can be shown by recent developments in four of the most celebrated tourist areas – the European Alps, the Mediterranean coast, the trekking regions of Nepal, and the English Lake District – each of which highlights the gravity of the present situation.

The Alps

Although it may not be immediately apparent to the winter visitor, the Alps have been steadily disfigured by tourism over the past thirty years. Now visited by 100 million people annually, they account for no less than one quarter of the world's annual tourism turnover. What was once

Europe's largest natural area and ecosystem has been steadily transformed into a vast tourist playground.

Skiing has of course been the principal cause of this dramatic change. Its development has been stupendous, as is underlined by the fact that the 3,000 cable railways and 13,000 ski lifts in the Alps together enable 1.3 billion 'transports' to be made annually. This means that in four years the equivalent of the entire world's population could have been on the Alpine ski slopes. But other activities have also become popular, among them paragliding, white water rafting, mountain biking and of course rock climbing.

The effect on the Alpine landscape, wildlife and local people has been devastating. Forests have been destroyed, soil eroded, wildlife disturbed. More than half the species of the region's flora and fauna are threatened or disappearing. The demand for skiing has led to the construction of hundreds of buildings, many of them revealed as blots on the landscape once the snow disappears. Traditional activities are vanishing as local people leave the region, no longer able to live off the land. Meanwhile, the congestion and pollution caused by the growing number of tourists coming by car has transformed a region once famous for its clean air and peaceful landscape.

Preserving the Alps: Switzerland

The Alps are the most threatened mountain system in the world. The environmental partnership Alp Action brings together tourism authorities, mountain communities, scientists, environmental organisations, businesses and governments. Its aim is to encourage tourism based on quality and respect for nature by promoting sustainable development, and working to preserve the natural and cultural heritage of the Alps.

Its many practical projects include:
• Halting the depopulation of the Alps and the erosion of its traditions.
• Reviving ancient building crafts.
• Preserving the region's threatened ecosystem.
• Promoting rail transport and renewable sources of energy.
• Protecting the Alpine flora and fauna.

The Mediterranean

The shores of the Mediterranean and the surrounding districts attract over a third of the world's tourist trade, notably in the summer months. In 1990 around 100 million tourists visited the Mediterranean region, and this number is forecast to double by the year 2025 – or even quadruple in some forecasts.

It's here that the results of the boom in cheap package holidays, and the facilities that were built to meet the demand, can be seen most clearly. All along the coast, from Spain to Turkey, uncontrolled development of hundreds of tourist resorts has blighted what used to be an area of great natural beauty. The pursuit of quick profits on the part of some developers and tour operators has resulted in the creation of mile upon mile of hugely inappropriate, low-cost development, often with totally inadequate water, sewage and road facilities. A process that began in Spain and then Portugal soon spread to Italy and Greece, and has now reached parts of Turkey. By 1990, tourists were outnumbering inhabitants by a ratio of 4:3 in Spain, and by 3:2 in Portugal.

The cumulative effect on the environment has been devastating. Traffic congestion around the coastal resorts becomes worse each year, increasing the pollution in the atmosphere. Down at sea-level, the Mediterranean is now the dirtiest sea in the world, its beaches contaminated with litter and sewage, a few of its resorts breeding-grounds for dysentery, typhoid and cholera. Since 1960, more than a third of dunes on the Atlantic coast and almost two-thirds on Mediterranean coasts have been destroyed.

Not all of this is a direct consequence of the huge influx of tourists into the region. But some of the threats to the area's wildlife have certainly been linked to tourist developments. Dolphins have been harmed by trying to feed off litter such as plastic bags left on the beaches. The breeding grounds of the monk seal and nesting sites of the loggerhead sea turtle have both recently been threatened by the developers' actions, and have been the subject of vigorous campaigns by conservation bodies.

The immediate future seems to offer little respite. It's been estimated that, if present trends continue, as much as 95% of the Mediterranean Basin could be developed by the year 2030. The present figure of

320 million residents could grow to one of 500 million, with a further 200 million tourists pouring into the region, driving 150 million cars. The implications of such figures are horrendous.[2]

Trekking in Nepal

After Hinduism and Buddhism, Nepal's third religion is reckoned to be 'trekking tourism'. In 1970 the country received 1,500 tourists; by 1993 the number was approaching the 300,000 mark. A quarter of these visitors now come to follow one of the many trekking trails that wind across the deep valleys and snow-clad mountain ranges of this beautiful country. These have been dubbed the 'Kleenex trails', a label prompted by the tonnes of rubbish tourists leave by the wayside. The coming of the trekkers in their thousands over the last twenty years has transformed areas of Nepal such as Kathmandu, Annapurna and Everest, creating many intractable environmental problems.

One of the most severe has been the impact on Nepal's abundant forests, the source of 86% of its energy. Thousands of trees have been felled in order to build the lodges which the trekkers use for accommodation, and provide the hot water, heating and cooking facilities they demand. Statistics produced by local conservationists make for alarming reading.

- Nearly a million acres of forest – the equivalent of an area slightly larger than Hampshire – are cleared every year.
- A single trekking lodge may consume a hectare of virgin forest a year to cater for the needs of trekker tourists.
- One trekker consumes between 5 and 10 times more wood than a Nepali does.
- At the present rate of loss, the country's forests will have disappeared by the year 2000.

Tourism is a good foreign currency earner for Nepal, providing about a sixth of its earnings. But few local people seem to benefit financially from the tourists' presence. The World Wide Fund for Nature has estimated that less than 7% of the money spent by an average trekker gets through to the Nepalese in the villages; the rest is spent on imported goods, mainly from Western countries.

The rapid increase in tourism has had other effects. It has drawn workers away from the land, to take jobs catering for the tourists. The 70,000 trekkers a year need double that number of guides, porters and cooks to support their activities. Many Nepalese men have been attracted to these jobs, leaving their womenfolk to cope alone in the family home.

It's also said that foreign tourists have introduced a new spirit of acquisitiveness, and a 'fast-buck' mentality. Traditional houses have been modified and local handicrafts modernised in order to meet the demands of the tourists. Slowly but surely, the indigenous culture is being lost.[3]

The Lake District

Tourists come to the much-loved English Lake District to walk on the fells, sail boats, take a trip on a lake steamer, or visit the homes of literary figures such as Dorothy and William Wordsworth, John Ruskin and Beatrix Potter. Many also come in search of peace and quiet; but these are commodities that are becoming increasingly hard to find.

Around 20 million visits are made to the area every year. Most visitors come for the day, and travel by car. During the summer, lengthy traffic jams have become a feature on the roads around some of the most popular spots. But the biggest increase in traffic around Ambleside has been between November and February, as people try to avoid the peak period. The popularity of the area has led to more accommodation being opened up every year. Meanwhile, in some towns as many as 40% of houses are being used for only a part of the year as second homes. Time-share developments are also becoming established.

The damage to the physical environment has been considerable. For instance, the sole path up the spine of Helvellyn has gradually been widened by the pressure of walkers, so that it begins to resemble a trunk road. The National Trust, which owns a quarter of the Lake District National Park, now spends £3.5 million a year on landscape maintenance, which includes footpath repairs: 170,000 alone goes on employing four permanent footpath gangs.

The serenity of this beautiful region is also being disturbed by the increasing use of the Lakes for water sports. Power boats used for water-skiing are particularly disruptive to the quiet enjoyment of those visitors and local people who wish to walk, fish, sail or row. This clash of interests has led to the imposition of a 10mph speed limit on, for example, Coniston Water and Ullswater, which has effectively banned people from using speed boats on them. Attempts by the authorities to impose a similar ban on Lake Windermere have met with opposition from some local businesses, from watersports enthusiasts, and from the Sports Council. In the summer of 1994 the conflict led to a lengthy planning inquiry.

The number of visitors to the Lake District has become so great that several radical ideas for controlling them are now being seriously discussed by the planning authorities. These include imposing quotas on visitor numbers, the exclusion of coaches from particular roads, and charging for entry to certain areas at peak visiting times during the summer.

Alternative destinations

But it's not just in the better known places in Europe and elsewhere that these kinds of problems are occurring. More and more people are now travelling further and further afield in search of something different or more active. It may be a holiday in the more remote wilderness areas of an African country, a visit to Iceland, or a trip to an island such as Bali in Indonesia. Even a region as apparently unwelcoming as Antarctica attracts some six thousand tourists a year.

A new set of countries has also become accessible to tourists during the 1990s, as a result of the fundamental political changes that have taken place in Eastern Europe. The opening up of the former East Germany and Czechoslovakia, Poland, Hungary, Romania, Bulgaria and the Baltic States has increased holiday travel both into and out of these countries. Yet though many areas there are so far unspoilt by tourist developments, pressures are already being exerted by foreign companies. In Estonia, for example, Danish and German firms are trying to persuade local authorities to let them build hotels, golf courses and tennis courts along a fine piece of coastline within the Lahemaa National Park.[4]

The arrival of mass tourism in certain developing countries has brought problems to the economic and social relationships between the visitors and local people. Where the costs of tourism have clearly outweighed the benefits, some people have made a link between tourism and colonialism. They quote figures such as those from the World Bank, which has estimated that 55 cents of every tourist dollar go back to developed countries, and that local inhabitants receive as little as ten cents of local revenue generated.

But the worst and most degrading human consequence of tourism has been its effect upon the lives of hundreds of thousands of women and children, who are being lured, abducted or sold into prostitution in countries such as Thailand, Sri Lanka and the Philippines, Taiwan and Vietnam, in order to feed the sexual demands of tourists. Most of these come from the 'developed' countries (including the UK), where tour operators openly advertise sex holidays. Of the 160 men who have been arrested in the last three years, 12% were British.

An international campaign against the trade, prompted by the organisation End Child Prostitution in Asian Tourism, has made some progress. In Australia, France, Germany, Norway and Sweden, legislation has now been introduced which allows citizens of those countries who

Death as a Tourist Attraction: Bali, Indonesia

Tourism contributes around 20% to the economy of Bali, a small island in the Indonesian archipelago. In 1968 there were 5,000 foreign visitors a year; by 1989 the figure was approaching 450,000. The target in the present five-year plan is an annual increase of 15%.

The recent dramatic rise in tourist activity, especially in the resorts in the south of the island, is putting increasing pressure on scarce resources, where tourism is competing with agriculture for land and water. It has also brought problems of coastal erosion, waste disposal and uneven development.

Most Bali residents in this predominantly Moslem country are Hindu. Visitors are attracted not only by the well-known handicrafts but by the cultural traditions of the Balinese, to the extent that even cremations have become a tourist attraction.

sexually abuse children overseas to be prosecuted. Belgium, Japan, New Zealand and the USA are considering bringing in such a law, but the UK, to its shame, is not. In the summer of 1994 the government refused to accept an amendment to the Criminal Justice Bill which would have introduced such legislation. Meanwhile, despite concern within some of the governments of the countries where such offences are taking place, there has been a general reluctance to prosecute. One of the prime reasons for this is acknowledged to be the fear of frightening off potential tourists.

These examples highlight the capacity of tourism to destroy people, places and cultures. Today, as members of the global village, we know more about this process than we did even a quarter of a century ago. It was then, in the early 1970s, that certain groups and individuals, concerned about the adverse effects of mass tourism and wanting to find alternatives that would be less destructive, first began to discuss the notion of what we now call 'sustainable tourism'.

Managing Visitors

The Peak Tourism Partnership

The early start had been worthwhile. Until I reached the top of Mam Tor, I had passed perhaps half a dozen walkers. In such rare solitude, I had been able to absorb at leisure the breathtaking quiet of the hills around Hope Valley.

It had been two hours of steadily changing perspectives. First the delicate but lush May countryside rising above Hope village, with its sporadically wooded slopes and busy farms. Then on to the open hillside, and the steady climb up to Losehill, the larks calling insistently above me. It was a bright, sharp day, with the occasional cloud mottling the nearest dales. Reaching the top, I looked around at the stunning panorama all about me: Edale Head, Back Tor, Win Hill, even Longstone Moor some eight miles away. Apart from two slow-moving specks on the rim of one hill across the dale, there was not a human being in sight.

But once I struck west across to Mam Tor and got past Hollins Cross, it was a very different story. I exchanged greetings with an increasing number of walkers: not just loners and couples, but small groups, some with frisky children, others with dogs, everything from golden labradors to poodles. Most of them, I assumed, were day trippers from places such as Manchester, Sheffield, Nottingham, Derby or Stoke, just a few of the many thousands who regularly escape from the city into the Peak District at summer weekends.

As I approached the highest point of Mam Tor, I came across some striking evidence of the pressure the many thousands of visitors put on the area. Half a dozen young men, who turned out to be working for the National Trust, were repairing the footpath that leads to the top. Using local gritstone, they were laying down flagstones over the well-trodden earth, and seeding the bare brown patches that still protruded on either side. It's apparently an expensive business: nearby, perched on vast pallets, are scores of stone slabs taken from closed-down mills in Yorkshire. One of the gang told me they had been flown in by helicopter to avoid damaging the area further.

The repair work is all too necessary. Mam Tor, a Celtic name meaning 'mother mountain', was an Iron Age hillfort and possibly a Bronze Age settlement. It's known locally as 'Shivering Mountain', because of the enormous section of black shale that has slipped away from one side, leaving a dramatically sheer cliff face, as if a giant hand had scooped out an enormous slab of rock in one swift gesture. Even now blocks of rock and the occasional sheep fall down on to the cracked road below, permanently closed some time ago.

Rock formations at Kinder Scout in the Peak District, Derbyshire.

Every year a quarter of a million people pass across Mam Tor, destroying the vegetation and exposing the topsoil, which is then swept away by wind and rain. The National Trust team is working both to protect an important archaeological site, and to heal the scars of erosion that visitors inflict on the area. It's clearly a formidable task. 'And even now people still go round the path,' one volunteer told me ruefully.

The human pressures on Mam Tor are typical of those facing many areas within the 555 square miles of the Peak District National Park. Some 18.5 million people live within sixty miles of here. An estimated 22 million visits are made every year, mostly by day trippers looking for a taste of the moorlands and dales, the reservoirs and rivers, and the historic houses and gentle market towns that characterise this stunningly beautiful upland region.

Yet this is not a new phenomenon. 'When I was a lad, there were many more people coming here,' explained Tony Singelton, who was born in the area, and at whose guest-house near Hope I had stayed the previous night. 'But in those days they came by train and bus, so it didn't seem so many. Nowadays most of them come by car, and that's a real headache in the summer.'

Increasing traffic congestion during summer weekends was one of the problems that prompted the setting up of the Peak Tourism Partnership in the summer of 1992. Another was the increasing amount of damage being done to the landscape, especially the footpaths, and that inflicted on plant life and farm property.

As a first step, the partnership has singled out two contrasting areas of the Peak District for special attention. One is the Roaches in the south-west of the park, a series of ridges and outcrops easily accessible from the Pottery towns. Large numbers of people are descending on the area and causing damage to a place which is environmentally sensitive, and which includes many Sites of Special Scientific Interest.

Much of the second is included in my day's walk, and encompasses the parishes of Castleton, Hope and Edale, all within relatively easy reach of Sheffield. Around 2 million visitors annually come to this part of the park, to explore the mines and caves scattered around Castleton, to visit the remains of the Norman Peveril Castle standing above the town, to amble through the lush Hope Valley, to venture on to Mam Tor, or to tackle the lengthy Pennine Way which begins its route at Edale.

Created as a three-year national pilot project, the partnership's stated aim is to develop a programme 'that will ensure sustainable tourism activity and an integrated approach to visitor management throughout the Peak District'. Now, more than half-way through its life, how has the rhetoric been translated into action?

The key to much of its early work, according to project manager Chris Lewis, has been the participation of the local community. Some 38,000 people live and work in the Peak District. Any scheme that attempts to solve its tourist-related problems needs to involve them from the start. Such a process was adopted for both the pilot areas. In the case of Castleton, Hope and Edale, around sixty people from all sections of the community were invited early on to a workshop at Hope Valley College, at which they could put forward what they saw as the problems, and air their views on how to tackle them. They were chosen following the 'mapping' of the local population by specialists in community involvement, to identify the opinion formers.

'Despite the national park's good conservation record, there's a deep suspicion of planners and plans, because many local people have had run-ins over planning applications,' Chris Lewis says. 'Traditionally, in tourism, there's been a lack of integrated planning, so that communities are generally faced with plans that have already been developed by outsiders, with little or no local involvement. There's the usual public meeting, to which nobody comes, and then all hell breaks loose. We've tried to break new ground by involving local people from the outset. Initially there was a blood-letting phase, with people sounding off about everything. In that situation you get as many opinions as there are people. But it had the beneficial effects of bringing people in the three parishes together, and getting an airing for the main issues that were worrying people.'

The next stage was the setting up of a thirty-strong working group, consisting of councillors at parish, district and county level, agencies involved in the area, and representatives of the local community, tourism businesses, and user groups. An important feature was the fact that half of the group worked or lived in the area. Stuart Elliott, a local farmer who was made chairman, says: 'It's not often that you have a chance to be a part of your own destiny. Usually you just get a public meeting, and that's it. This was different, it got us all round the table talking to each other.'

Consultants were then employed to work with the group to produce a draft plan. The general feeling was that the plan reflected the key issues, and managed to balance the needs of local people with those of the area's visitors and of the environment. There was some resistance from local shopkeepers, but a parish appraisal in Castleton which got a 90% response rate showed that most people were in favour of some kind of visitor management scheme, since it was clearly becoming increasingly difficult for tourists to park, or even just move around. The next stage will involve agreeing how the proposals should be implemented, and bringing together a funding package from national, regional and local sources.

Another part of the partnership's programme has entailed setting up a local tourism heritage trust. The idea is to involve those who benefit from tourism in the raising of funds for conservation work – such as mending drystone walls or restoring damaged footpaths – and to help maintain the facilities used by visitors to an area. Visitors are encouraged to donate money to the trust, which then regularly distributes funds to conservation and visitor management projects that enhance the attractiveness of the area.

Such a scheme may not immediately meet with favour amongst the public. But research carried out by the partnership in the Hope Valley showed that a surprising 73% of those questioned were in favour of the idea. As a result, the trust is being launched with two pilot projects. One involves visitors giving voluntary contributions at car parks in the Hope Valley, by inserting money into slot machines. The other entails adding a voluntary 50p to a £25 accommodation bill in certain hotels, guest houses, activity centres and hostels. The group is clear that the public have to know what projects they are helping to pay for.

Interpretation is another issue being tackled. The aim is to encourage visitors to learn more about the natural environment of the Peak District and the area's rich history and culture, in the hope that they will be more likely to want to conserve and enhance it. The partnership, with the help of the Centre for Environmental Interpretation at Manchester Metropolitan University, formed an interpretation group which has devised a statement of intent and good practice. This has already been adopted by the national park as well as by the surrounding local authorities. Finally, six local integrated planning groups have been set up around the Peak, to develop plans locally.

The partnership is also looking at the difficult issue of marketing, which is generally seen as a tool for maximising visitor numbers, but can equally be a valuable tool in the promotion of sustainable tourism, and for matching visitors to appropriate places. For an area as popular as the Peak District, strategies are having to be devised to channel people into the less developed areas. 'De-marketing' may, for example, mean sometimes leaving some of the 'honeypots' out of the brochure. 'You can have all the best-laid plans for visitor management in the world,' says Chris Lewis, 'but they'll be of no use at all if the private and public marketeers are going in the opposite direction.'

The little town of Castleton is certainly classed as one of the region's 'honeypot' areas. After leaving Mam Tor and striking out along the edge of the dramatically narrow Winnats Pass, I ended my walk on the hillside next to Peveril Castle, and descended into the town below. It was late afternoon and the narrow pavements, the gift shops, the pubs and tea-rooms of this attractive medieval town were crammed tight with dozens of fellow-tourists. I commented on the crowds to a man selling ice-cream in the post office. 'Busy!' he snorted. 'You should have been here at the Bank Holiday. It was sheer murder. If you want to come to Castleton, come during the week.' I might take his advice next time.

While the involvement of local communities in the Peak Tourism Partnership appears to have been a success, there is a clear danger that people in the area will feel disillusioned if nothing ultimately comes of the plans they have spent so much time and effort in devising. Stuart Elliott is blunt about the consequence of failure: 'Expectations have been raised,' he says. 'The reaction will be quite dramatic if no funding comes. People are likely to say, "We've bitten the bullet, and there's the report gathering dust, so don't ever come and ask us to do this again."'

2 Sustainable Tourism

'Take nothing but photographs; leave nothing but footprints; kill nothing but time.'

Tourist motto

One of the original proponents of the basic ideas inherent in sustainable tourism was the Swiss academic Jost Krippendorf, author of the influential book *The Holiday Makers*, and one of the first to draw attention to the damage being done to the Swiss Alps by tourist developments. He argued vigorously that mass tourism was gradually destroying everything that it touched – the environment, the economy, the host country and its people, even the tourists themselves – and that a better way had to and could be found.

Despite the intense debates over the ensuing years about a host of environmental issues, the question of the impact of tourism was largely ignored except by a tiny minority, who continued to try to bring the issue to wider public attention. But it was the focus on sustainability in the Brundtland Report *Our Common Future*, published in 1987, which started to bring about change. Here sustainable development was defined as 'development that meets the needs of the present without compromising the ability of future generations to meet their own needs'. The report made no significant reference to tourism. But since its publication, as concern has grown about the effect of our continuing misuse of the earth's resources, and about the part played by tourism in this process, the links between development and tourism have increasingly been made.

One of the consequences of the publication of *Our Common Future* was another report, *Caring for the Earth*, which mapped out a wide-ranging set of principles for sustainable living. These were to prove influential in the developing arguments about the impact of tourism. The report, which was prepared by the World Conservation Union, the World

Wide Fund for Nature and the United Nations Environment Programme, for consideration by the Earth Summit in Rio in 1992, suggested that we need to:

- Respect and care for the community of life.
- Improve the quality of human life.
- Conserve the Earth's vitality and diversity.
- Minimise the depletion of non-renewable resources.
- Keep within the Earth's carrying capacity.
- Change personal attitudes and practices to adopt the ethic of sustainable living.
- Enable communities to care for their own environments.
- Provide a national framework for integrating development and conservation.

At Rio, effectively for the first time on an international scale, the link between development and conservation was broadly accepted. It was now recognised that the two need not be in opposition to each other, but are and should be intertwined. By now the negative impact of tourism, including its growing threat to the aims and practice of many conservation bodies, was becoming better and more widely understood, in developed and developing countries alike. The high-profile debate about sustainable living soon encompassed the tourism issue, and the notion of sustainable tourism came on to the agenda.

The new tourism

In recent years various terms have been used to describe this newer form of tourism. The most unsatisfactory of these is 'green tourism', an increasingly meaningless catch-all phrase which is all too often used as a cosmetic or misleading label – especially by those who have something to sell. Within the tourism industry there is a further problem: in many people's minds it appears, incorrectly, to mean the same as 'rural tourism'. Either way, it's a term much used within tourism, and by many people whose work or ideas feature in this book.

Another popular term is 'alternative tourism', which conveys some meaning of difference to mainstream practice, but doesn't include any sense of the activity itself, or what its principles may be. Another label that is sometimes used is 'responsible tourism'. This to my mind has a rather sanctimonious and exclusive ring to it, and implies that all other tourism is totally irresponsible.

The term 'ecotourism' is a more meaningful one. It's most commonly applied to the type of holiday which enables tourists to have much more direct contact with nature than usual. Ecotourism generally means a visit to one of the more remote areas, where you can observe animals and birds in their natural habitat, examine the flora and fauna at first hand, or have direct, unmediated contact with a local community. Such tourism may involve studying the behaviour of the big game in a Kenyan safari park, taking part in some serious birdwatching in the Seychelles, or observing the whales off Greenland. It's a type of holiday that's becoming increasingly popular, and the number of organisations catering for the ecotourist is growing rapidly. Many of the holidays have a strong conservation element built into them: simply by going to these remote places, the argument runs, you're helping to preserve them in their natural or semi-natural state. In some places tourists are even taking part in conservation efforts, working alongside local people.

Ecotourism in action in the Chitwan National Park, Nepal.

Yet ecotourism may simply be a way of describing a tourist develop-ment that happens to be in a 'natural' setting. It can also very easily have its own kind of negative effects. For example, the conserving of an area of land so that it can be of use to tourists may be the means whereby local people are prevented from using it for the basic essentials of living – and sometimes even survival.

It has also been argued that the 'ecotourist', by going to areas where few tourists may have ventured before, is simply paving the way for more and more people to visit what are often very fragile environments. When this happens, more damage may be caused in the long term by the ecotourist effectively pushing back the frontiers of mass tourism than by the tourist holidaying in a well-established but under-used resort.

Finally, there is 'sustainable tourism'. One of its more concise and helpful definitions is that used by the Federation of Nature and National Parks in Europe, which recently commissioned a working group to look at the phenomenon of tourism in protected areas. In its ensuing report *Loving Them to Death?*, the group defined sustainable tourism as 'all forms of tourism development, management and activity which maintain the environmental, social and economic integrity and well-being of natural, built and cultural resources in perpetuity'.[1] This seems as good a definition as any against which to measure different kinds of tourist activity.

Versions of sustainability

Like many a new idea, sustainable tourism is interpreted in many different ways. Problems arise because different people and agencies see the term in different lights, or from different perspectives, which may be incompatible.

Definitions vary according to circumstances. In a much-visited fragile area of the countryside the focus may be on sustaining the physical environment by taking steps to prevent long-term damage. In another place the accent may be on sustaining the viability of the local economy, or maintaining the authenticity of the community's artistic traditions. For an officer in a national park, sustainable tourism may mean achieving a proper balance for visitors between access and enjoyment; for a small hotelier it may simply be a question of wanting to ensure the family business survives another year.

Some observers feel that the concept is only being superficially grasped, or used for political convenience. One of these is Ann Clegg, a college lecturer in tourism. 'There is a lot of hot air, many words, but not a consensus as to what is really being talked about,' she says. 'The whole concept is being bandied about in local authority strategy plans throughout the length of Britain. But in my experience few tourism officers really understand what it is about or where it has come from, but find it a useful way of getting councillors on their side when they want to get over the Not-In-My-Back-Yard problems.'[2]

This is a pessimistic, even cynical analysis, but also a useful reminder that it's deeds rather than words that ultimately count. The projects in the UK and Ireland described later in this book might not all pass a rigorous sustainability test in every detail. Yet they still represent the vanguard of the movement as it stands at present, and this alone makes them worthy of examination.

Revitalising the Economy: Cyprus

The Laona Project is based in the Akamas Peninsula, the north-western tip of Cyprus. Its aim is to help local people protect the region by introducing non-intrusive, sustainable tourism.

The project has been offering grants and low-interest loans to villagers to renovate their traditional properties for tourist accommodation or other small-scale enterprises. It has paid for a facility – a museum, a visitor centre – selected by each of the communities in which it works.

Adrian Akers-Douglas of the project says: 'We had to overcome widespread scepticism from people who felt that their customs and lifestyles were worthless and of no interest to sophisticated foreigners, or, worse, that we were proposing to reduce the local population to some form of exhibit in a theme park. But once the facilities started to come on line, and people could see the benefits of high-quality, special-interest tourism, most of this suspicion disappeared.'

Maintaining the balance

Different countries emphasise different aspects of sustainable tourism, depending on the state of their economy, environment and tourism industry. In Britain in the late 1980s there was growing concern about the effect an increasing number of visitors was having on parts of the countryside, on certain heritage sites, and on many historic towns and cities. Finally in the summer of 1990 the government, through the Department of Employment, set up a 'task force' to look at the problem and come up with recommendations.

Its task was 'to examine the scale and nature of the problems caused by visitor numbers at tourist sites and areas, and to examine the environmental and other benefits which tourism brings to such areas'. Based on experience in the UK and elsewhere, it was also required 'to draw up guidance on how the tourism industry and other agencies might ensure that their present activities and policies, as well as future tourism developments, are in harmony with both the need to conserve and preserve the environment, and the need to serve the well-being of host populations.'

In its report, *Tourism and the Environment: Maintaining the Balance*, published the following spring, the task force decided the concept of sustainability was the key to a more productive and harmonious relationship between what it identified as the three key elements in the tourism equation: the visitor, the host community, and the place. It said it was 'looking to achieve a situation which can be maintained without depleting the resource, cheating the visitor, or exploiting the local population'.

It highlighted five central problems: overcrowding, traffic congestion, wear and tear, inappropriate development, and conflicts with the local community. It suggested various ways of tackling these problems, and came up with recommendations. These included the setting up of several pilot projects to show how good 'visitor management' could be achieved. It also concluded that existing resources were inadequate for the promotion of sustainable tourism, and made suggestions as to how the additional money might be raised.

The report also listed seven principles for sustainable tourism. These were:

1 The environment has an intrinsic value which outweighs its value as a tourism asset. Its enjoyment by future generations and its long-term survival must not be prejudiced by short-term considerations.

2 Tourism should be recognised as a positive activity, with the potential to benefit the community and the place as well as the visitor.

3 The relationship between tourism and the environment must be managed so that it is stable in the long term. Tourism must not be allowed to damage the resource, prejudice its future enjoyment, or bring unacceptable impacts.

4 Tourism activities and developments should respect the scale, nature and character of the place in which they are sited.

5 In any location, harmony must be sought between the needs of the visitor, the place and the host community.

6 In a dynamic world some change is inevitable, and change can often be beneficial. Adapting to change, however, should not be at the expense of any of these principles.

7 The tourism industry, local authorities and environmental agencies all have a duty to respect the above principles, and to work together to achieve their practical realisation.

The report suggested that all tourism activities involve three elements: the place being visited, the local community, and the tourists themselves. The relationship between them is crucial, and underpins the nature of the experience people have as tourists. But each raises different issues and questions in relation to sustainable tourism and how it can best be achieved, which are worth considering in some detail.

The place

It's important that the environment of the place being visited is looked after and treated as sensitively as possible. In order that this can be done, consideration needs to be given to a number of factors:

Carrying capacity. The carrying capacity of a place – essentially, the number of visitors it can take – is determined by many factors. They include its location and size; the presence of wildlife there; the nature of the activity undertaken by the visitor; and the fragility of its environment.

Keeping Control: The Seychelles

The government of this small republic exercises close control over tourism, which is becoming increasingly popular on its 115 islands. Its restrictive measures, designed to encourage sustainable tourism, include:

- Designating nearly half the land as national park.
- Putting a ceiling on the number of beds on the three largest islands.
- Forbidding any hotel to be built higher than a palm tree.
- Confining motorised water sports to just a few beaches.
- Encouraging tourists to travel by bicycle or ox-cart to their hotel.
- Forbidding motorcycles and camping.
- Banning land sales to foreigners.
- Keeping three of the islands as bird sanctuaries, to which visits are strictly rationed.

A question often asked is 'How many people can a place reasonably hold before it becomes too crowded?' Of course a lot depends on how you define 'crowded', since it's a concept that can change dramatically according to the location. But it's precisely because this question of 'carrying capacity' has rarely been put until recently that so many places have become 'honeypots', and the pleasure of visiting them has been diminished. What delight is there in gazing up at Michelangelo's work on the ceiling of the Sistine Chapel, when you're wedged in with hundreds of others trying to do the same? Where is the pleasure in visiting the Giant's Causeway, when the unique volcanic rocks you have come to see are covered with other tourists?

Determining the 'carrying capacity' of a place is crucial if sustainability is to be achieved. But such decisions are not straightforward: they will vary from place to place, depending on whether it is well established, a new attraction or development, or in the process of change or adaptation.

Physical damage. Many sites around the world have suffered damage over the years, sometimes irreparably. At Stonehenge in Wiltshire, for instance, the stones are now closed off because of erosion. At the celebrated Lascaux Caves in France, the astonishing prehistoric frescoes were suffering so much damage from the carbon dioxide created by visitors, that a facsimile of the caves had to be built nearby to stand in for the original. If such damage is occurring, how can it be reduced or eliminated? The problem may be the volume of visitors, or their concentration at certain times or places. Various measures have been used to combat the problem, including the closing off of fragile areas, either temporarily or permanently; the introduction of entry charges or advanced booking; or the staggering of the times at which visitors are allowed access to an area or site.

Transport. Cars are still the most popular form of transport for most visitors to most places. But the road networks around many attractions, especially those in the countryside, were just not designed to cope with great quantities of traffic. The result is congestion, pollution of the atmosphere, high levels of noise, or massive car parks that spoil the very view you've come to see. So persuading people to leave their cars elsewhere can be critical for the sustainability of both the place itself and the surrounding area. This can be encouraged by siting car parks at some distance from the attraction, or by creating 'pinch points' to prevent access for coaches.

Wildlife. If wildlife is present on the site or in the area, then its welfare needs to be carefully considered. Nature conservation is a key element in sustainable tourism. Again, various measures have served to protect the wildlife in well-established areas. In many nature reserves, for example, visitors are severely restricted during the breeding season. But new developments also create problems: for instance, many of the marinas being built in estuaries in Britain are posing a severe threat to the wildlife there.

Buildings. Many of the more popular visitor attractions in the UK are now constructing visitor centres, which aim to help with information, interpretation and education about the place being visited. It's important that such buildings – as well as any other facilities designed to meet the needs of tourists – are designed not to intrude on but to harmonise with their surroundings. This is especially important in relation to the scale of the building and the sensitive use of materials. In many cases this kind of harmony has been achieved by adapting older, sometimes derelict buildings for other uses. In other cases, a modern building can be perfectly appropriate.

The local community

Local people are often the first to suffer from the negative effects of tourism. The arrival of hundreds of tourists can be a severe intrusion in their lives, especially when the visitors outnumber the locals several times over, as happens in many country villages, small seaside resorts or remote areas. Noise, litter, vandalism and traffic congestion can breed resentment and anger in a community where tourism has got out of hand. Local people are also often left out of discussions about a new tourist development, or about changes to an existing site or area. This can result in anger and frustration, and even hostility towards the incoming tourists. To be viable in the long term, any tourist initiative or development has to gain and keep the active support of the local community. Several commentators have observed that sustainability in rural projects, for example, is highly dependent on the effective participation of local people. Harmony rather than hostility is needed, to keep any negative impact to a minimum, and to create as many benefits as possible for the local community.

Participation. This is especially important where a new tourist development is being created, or a new strategy being devised to cope with an unacceptably high number of visitors coming to an area. Where consultation does take place, it is often by means of a local forum, which gives all the parties involved – community groups, landowners, planners and tourist agencies – a chance to air their views and hear those of other people. This can lead to plans being modified to take into account local opinion or feelings. Change is rarely acceptable to everyone in a community, especially where there may be a clash of interests. But the very fact that people are involved from the beginning makes it more likely that the outcome will be accepted.

Employment. Tourism can be a positive force in creating jobs for local people. This is noticeably the case in rural areas, where farming subsidies are now in decline. The existence or development of a place that is popular with tourists not only provides direct employment; it also means that visitors will spend money in the local shops, pubs, cafés and restaurants, thereby helping the local economy. But tourism can also have an unsettling effect on local communities, since many of the jobs it provides are seasonal and low-paid, and may offer no long-term security. If too many people are drawn into the tourist trade and away from jobs that meet a community's basic needs, the quality of life can be adversely affected. Care needs to be taken to find a balance, to ensure that a sudden surge in tourism-related jobs does not upset the local economy, that a place does not suddenly become a tourism monoculture.

Preferential treatment. Many historic sites in the UK have made special arrangements with the local community, which allow them reductions on ticket prices, or the chance to use facilities at special rates. This can enable people to identify what may be a national attraction as something that also more obviously belongs to their community.

The tourists

Whether as individuals or in groups, the attitude of tourists both to the place they are visiting and to the people who live and work there is crucial if sustainable tourism is to be achieved. If respect, care and tolerance are the hallmarks of their behaviour towards people and places alike, then the experience can be a fruitful, positive and enjoyable one for all parties. But if the visit is characterised by a lack of sympathy with or understanding of the local people, or carelessness about damaging the environment or over-using local resources, then the loss can be considerable.

Sustainable tourism means encouraging people to act in certain ways, whether they are looking for total relaxation on holiday, taking a day trip to the coast or countryside, or indulging in an active adventure trip in some far-off wilderness. The following points are among those made in some of the many 'good tourist' codes that are being devised in different countries:

- Using public transport, or other means of travel that are environmentally friendly, such as cycling or, best of all, walking, helps to lessen traffic congestion in popular places, as well as reduce the amount of pollution caused by car use.

- Avoiding the peak times of the year or the week for a visit or holiday helps to ease overcrowding, and lessens any physical damage to the environment.

- Avoiding the honeypot areas can often provide an equally pleasurable experience, since there are many places off the beaten track that can match such attractions, while offering more space to the visitor.

- Treating the physical environment with care means not leaving litter behind, keeping off areas not open to the public, staying on footpaths or bridleways in the countryside, and being sensitive to the presence of wildlife.

- Considering the needs and rights of people living in the area involves respecting their privacy and their property, and their desire to live without interference from curious, noisy or insensitive visitors.

- Learning about the culture, language, history and geography of the place being visited can make it easier to make contact with local people, which can help to reduce the hostility which can build up between them and visitors.

- Such hostility can also be avoided or reduced by a recognition and tolerance of the different customs, codes of dress and behaviour of the local community.

- Buying local products and eating in locally owned cafés and restaurants can help to support the local economy, and ensure that more of the proceeds from tourism stay in the area, rather than go to outside individuals or companies.

- Using local resources sparingly means that more of them are available to local people during the rest of the year.

- Respecting the culture of a locality involves separating the authentic artistic experiences being offered from the phoney or 'adapted' ones created merely for tourists.

Such considerations are relevant to tourist activity in all kinds of places. But perhaps nowhere are they more critical than in the countryside, where so much land is now under threat from so many different quarters.

Pulling Together

The Isle of Purbeck

It is, there's no doubt about it, a gem of a bay. Looking down from the high, crumbling chalk cliffs on to the oyster shape of Lulworth Cove, I feel pleased that over the centuries the sea has managed to win at least one of its battles with the Portland stone that runs along this exquisite stretch of the Dorset coast.

Within the sheltered cove lie anchored a scattering of small yachts, dinghies, fishing boats and the occasional motor boat, interspersed with blue and red buoys, glanced here and there by the bright May sun. For a moment the tranquil scene is broken by the sudden appearance of a pleasure steamer, which stops briefly at the edge of the bay. A man booms out information about its history through a loudspeaker, before the steamer backs out again into open water, and heads over to Weymouth.

Walking up here on the cliffs – used for most of the year by the army as a practice firing range, but accessible today, though nearly deserted – the feeling is one of calm and space. But this is deceptive, as you quickly realise if you look across to the cliff on the other side of the cove. There an almost unbroken line of people is moving relentlessly, like an unending snake, up the steep and clearly eroded path to Durdle Door, determined in their hundreds to catch a glimpse of another unique formation that the sea has carved out of the local stone.

Below them, out of sight from our own cliff path, is the tiny entrance to Lulworth Cove where my friend and I began our visit earlier in the day. The narrow lane leading down to the enclosed shingle beach was awash with Bank Holiday visitors, the beach sandals and flamboyant T-shirts

Corfe Castle in the Isle of Purbeck.

outnumbering the staid shorts and heavy boots of the serious walkers. On each side of the lane stood the paraphernalia of seaside tourism: small booths and huts selling beach balls, cheap bright clothing, meat pies and ice cream. On the stone steps at the foot of the cliff path a tattoo'd man sat by a small sign: 'Toenails painted, any design, £2.' In the middle of all this commerce stood a small hut, in which the Dorset Nature Conservation Trust was trying to interest visitors in a small exhibition about the geology and history of the area.

Lulworth Cove, like many other small but beautiful places along England's south coast, has a visitor problem. Nearly half a million visits are made here every year. Over the last two summers repairs have had to be made to the badly eroded footpaths that wind up and along the cliffs. The car park – actually a huge sloping field stretching up and away inland – is often full to overflowing, as it is on this early summer Sunday. At such times it becomes a severe intrusion on the lovely and dramatic landscape.

But the problems at Lulworth merely reflect what is happening throughout the popular Dorset peninsula that constitutes the Isle of Purbeck, over 50% of which lies within the Dorset Area of Outstanding Natural Beauty. Four and half million visits are made here every year, a figure predicted to grow to five million by the end of the century. Most people come to see the National Trust's famous Corfe Castle, to relax on the sandy beaches of Studland Bay, to visit the Tank Museum at

Bovington Camp, or to sample the unique coastline and heathlands in and around Lulworth Cove. A proposed new trunk road is likely to make access to the region even easier than at present. Yet many locals in Purbeck feel that, in particular spots at certain times of the year, saturation point has already been reached.

Tourism is a crucial part of the local economy in many parts of the Isle, which is home to some 42,000 people. Encouraging more visitors to come here is obviously good for business, but the area is now seriously at risk because of the sheer numbers attracted to it. It was the realisation that action was urgently needed to protect it from long-term damage that led to the setting up of the Purbeck Heritage Committee.

'People were almost in despair. They were saying, How can we go on like this?' recalls Colin Bonsey, chairman of the committee. 'The way things were going, we realised it was only a matter of time before Purbeck became the victim of its own beauty unless something was done to save it.' The idea of an action committee was initially discussed amongst a hard core of representatives from the district and county councils and the Countryside Commission. Others – from the National Trust, English Nature, the tourism industry, local authorities, and local landowner and farmer organisations – were drawn in, and the committee was established in the autumn of 1993, initially for two years.

Its task is to work out a strategy for the area for the next ten years, and decide how best to put it into effect. From the start, the aim has been to work closely with local people, to make the committee a 'factory of inspiration and action' rather than a talking shop, as so many committees become. With this in mind, one of its first initiatives was to set up a Purbeck Forum, through which people from a range of local organisations could make their views known and offer ideas for action.

Representatives from all the many interest groups in Purbeck were invited to attend the forum. The first two meetings showed clearly the high level of interest amongst local people, with 80 turning up on each occasion and numbers having to be restricted. At the end of the first meeting people were still talking intensely. The second was an all-day workshop session, at which the various representatives were mixed up into groups and invited to discuss particular issues.

'It was a good way of allowing people to get their views across,' says Alison Turnock, Purbeck's heritage officer. 'But the workshop was also successful in getting them to make contact with each other – landowners with tourism people, and so on. It got people together who hadn't talked to each other much recently – in one case for fifteen years. Half of the problem with dealing with these kinds of issues is getting people to understand the other person's point of view.'

Many ideas were thrown up at the meetings, and some were incorporated into the draft strategy. Most of the topics discussed came under one of three headings: conservation, tourism and visitor management, or transport. But because of the number of issues raised, it was decided to set up specialist groups to look at certain questions under a number of broad headings, such as Green Tourism or Education.

One of the problems for Purbeck is that most visitors come at the busiest times of the year, and descend on certain well-known spots. Corfe Castle, for example, attracts 163,000 visits a year, Studland Bay has 655,000, the Tank Museum 150,000, and Lulworth Cove 472,000. Yet there are many beautiful areas inland – old stone villages within the Purbeck Hills, for example – that are relatively neglected. So questions being considered by the Green Tourism group include how to persuade people to come and enjoy the Purbeck countryside as well as the beaches, historic sites and museums, or convince them that it's better to visit the honeypot areas out of season.

The majority of visitors come to Purbeck for the day, many driving in from Bournemouth or Poole, where they may already be on holiday. So one aim of the group is to get visitors to consider alternative forms of transport – for instance, to use the train for the day trips. This raises the issue of how Purbeck is marketed outside the area. One of the points that has emerged out of the forum is the feeling that the information about the Isle could be improved: transport alternatives need to be set out for potential visitors, and packages put together to make the use of trains and buses more attractive.

Transport is inevitably one of the thorniest of the many questions with which the committee is concerning itself, and one that has been the subject of concern for some time. Plans for a new trunk road from Poole, still being discussed, have divided local people. For many local businesses the increased access will be an asset; but in other respects there are widespread anxieties about the likely impact of yet more visitors. 'It just means more people will be able to come into Purbeck at a faster rate, only to meet bottlenecks further on,' says Alison Turnock.

The problem is exemplified by the situation at Corfe Castle, where visitors coming to see the celebrated Norman castle have to drive through the narrow streets of the village just to get to the car park. Meanwhile local residents and visitors are competing for the minimal parking space available elsewhere. The resulting congestion is frustrating for everyone, and has led to bad feeling about visitors within the village.

Discussions about alternative solutions to the village's problems pre-date the setting up of the heritage committee. But drawing different interest groups together has clearly helped to concentrate people's minds on the need for action. The National Trust has now bought the privately owned Castle View Café, which will release valuable parking space for coaches and cars. Next year a new, more scenic route to the village will be signposted, so that visitors can avoid the main road.

Meanwhile, the railway line from Swanage is being extended as far as Norden Halt in Corfe. The Swanage Railway Company has laid down the tracks and bought a second-hand platform, and the line will soon be open for use. This will allow new 'park and ride' arrangements to be set up, so encouraging more visitors to leave their cars in Swanage.

One project that has already come to fruition is the Purbeck Cycleway, which offers along its 47 miles a range of routes that take in some of the area's finest landscapes. Another idea being looked at is the possibility of raising money for conservation work directly from visitors. A number of alternatives are being considered, as is the question of whether donations should be compulsory or voluntary. A scheme involving a levy on accommodation would be one option, but would not affect the huge numbers of day visitors. A levy on parking would be another possibility. 'But we don't want people thinking that you're ripping them off by putting up the charge by 10p,' Alison Turnock says. 'They need to know that the money they give is going to the heritage committee for improvements to the area. There are also legal and technical difficulties.

So we have to think through carefully how we do it.'

The committee's work is made up of many threads, much of it involving building on previous discussions and initiatives. It has, for instance, involved itself in widening the scheme to bring about improvements to the seafront at Swanage, which formed part of the recent Purbeck Local Plan. Swanage, like many resorts established in Victorian times, has fallen on hard times since the boom in foreign holidays in the 1960s. 'Tourism there has been of the old bucket-and-spade variety, and no one wants that any more,' Colin Bonsey says. Now plans are in hand to restore the seafront area, including the pier, and to improve the appearance of the older part of the town, to attract holidaymakers back and help revive the local economy.

With many of the schemes that the committee has become involved with, its very existence, and the resulting pooling of resources, have helped to augment pressure for change, or speed up decision-making. But this has certainly not meant that everyone suddenly speaks with one voice – especially on an issue such as roads. 'We're not trying to get everyone to agree to everything,' Alison Turnock says. 'It's more about agreeing common objectives, and then deciding on a strategy.' That strategy, which she is now drafting, will shortly go out for consultation. It has, she says, been strongly influenced by the ideas and opinions that have come out of the forum meetings.

Local democracy seems to be working in Purbeck. Colin Bonsey believes there is a good reason for this. 'The mechanism is right, because it allows ideas to come from the bottom up, rather than be imposed by some outside authority,' he suggests. 'It has also allowed people in very opposite camps to sit down quite easily and talk to each other, rather than just score points as they normally tend to do.'

As to the committee's impact on the problems facing the area, he feels encouraged by progress so far. 'The public interest has been considerable, but it's early days yet. We don't expect immediate or spectacular change; it has to be a long-term job, and we have to do one thing at a time. But people are pulling together now, rather than fighting each other, and that has to be good for Purbeck.'

3 Country Matters

'Is there no nook of ground secure from rash assault?'

William Wordsworth on tourists

Tourism in the countryside is a particularly complex and emotive issue. It challenges our ideas about what gives the countryside its special quality. It raises questions about continuity and change, about our sense of place, about our feelings concerning the natural and the man-made, and our notion of what constitutes the national heritage.

As visitors to or holiday-makers in the countryside, we tend to look for certain experiences and sensations not available elsewhere. For the tourist in the UK, they may include the feeling of freedom and space to be found in a walk in the hills or over a mountain; the delight felt in observing the weathered architecture of an old village, or the view over a sheep-strewn valley criss-crossed by stone walls; an appreciation of the variety of trees and flowers to be found in a long-established woodland; the powerful historical pull of an ancient burial site; or the curiosity that makes us want to find out more about the local language, traditions and customs of an area.

In general we tend to like countryside that is familiar, ancient, unchanging, diverse and distinctive. We also want it to be 'unspoilt', but at the same time accessible to anyone who wants to enjoy it. But these sentiments can be in conflict with each other, and the clash between them fraught with difficulty. The ironic result of the increasing number of us who visit the countryside is the loss in some places of those very qualities that draw us there.

In the UK the sheer number of visitors is causing a wide range of problems. What precisely these are depends on the location:

• On the Norfolk Broads, the river banks are being eroded by the wash created by the large number of pleasure boats.

- On the Pennine Way, serious erosion has caused the path to be diverted in places as part of a £3 million repair programme.
- At Stonehenge in Wiltshire, the pressure of visitors has led to plastic grass being laid down around the stones.
- In Clovelly on the Devon coast, some of the 400,000 annual visitors to the village wander into residents' homes.
- In the Yorkshire Dales, increasing theft of limestone and wildflowers for garden use has led the park authorities to seek protection orders.

When rural tourism is being actively promoted, as it now is in the UK and many other European countries, there can be further problems. Conflicts can arise with or within the local community about what is appropriate for the area. Resentment can be aroused at the number of local houses being used by newcomers as second homes – in the Lake District it is now a third of the housing in some parishes – or time-share accommodation. Disturbance to wildlife habitats can become widespread. Increased noise can bedevil the lives of local people. And all the efforts to sell the charms of a place to potential visitors may result in the loss of that very distinctiveness that makes it unique.

Underlying all these problems is the fact that visiting the countryside has become an increasingly popular occupation in the UK. A Day Visits Survey organised by the Countryside Commission in the summer of 1993 graphically highlighted this situation. The researchers found that in England:

- Nearly six out of ten in the population visit the countryside (for Scotland and Wales the figure is five out of ten).
- Over one third of leisure visits are made to the countryside.
- Around a billion such visits are made in a full year.
- Four in ten visits take place at weekends.
- Walking is the most popular activity for countryside visitors (37%), followed by outdoor sports (12%).

National Parks

Problems caused by tourism can be particularly acute in the wilder, more remote areas. Many of the places where people are looking for the more adventurous type of holiday are protected areas, in some cases national or nature parks. But often there is pressure to establish facilities for tourists which are quite inappropriate. The growing popularity of motorised transport for recreation, bringing with it noise and pollution, has also put pressure on such environmentally sensitive regions. And the fact that most people travel there by car, often because of the lack of good public transport facilities, has inevitably led to congestion, increased levels of pollution, and the need to provide extra parking space.

It was in order both to preserve and enhance the beauty of these more vulnerable places, as well as to promote the enjoyment of them by the public, that national or nature parks were first established. The idea had its origins in the 1870s in the United States, where the new national park system brought together for the first time the notions of conservation, recreation and managed development. Those first parks were mainly set up to protect huge, uninhabited areas of land. In European and other countries where the idea has been taken up the accent has been on conserving 'protected landscapes', the definition for areas of natural beauty in which also people live and work.

The eleven national parks in England and Wales owe their origin to groups formed in the nineteenth century to protect the landscape, as well as to others which later fought for improved rights of access to wild and open country for those living in towns and cities. Because they are in areas of outstanding natural beauty, they tend to be among the most visited regions in the countryside. The Lake District, for instance, has 20 million visits a year, the North York Moors and Snowdonia 11 million, and the Yorkshire Dales 7.5 million. Between them the parks have a resident population of around a quarter of a million, whose interests have to be taken into account when the authorities are contemplating change or developments.

Visitors to the parks inevitably tend to congregate in a limited number of popular spots, thereby putting immense pressure on the landscape. For instance Dovedale, one of the limestone dales in the south of the Peak District National Park, attracts two million visitors a year, of whom 750,000 use the main footpath. On busy summer Sundays no less than two thousand people *an hour* can be crossing the river by the stepping stones. In Snowdonia, where half a million people a year reach the summit of Snowdon itself, the paths have been badly eroded, and access to certain parts has had to be limited. In the Norfolk Broads, Britain's newest national park in all but name, the banks of the region's rivers and broads are being gradually washed away by waves from motor boats, forcing the authority to shore them up with unsightly sheet-steel piling, so preventing the wildlife from using the banks.

Traffic problems have also loomed very large. In 1991 the report on national parks *Fit for the Future* called for experimental car-free zones. The moment for these seems to be fast approaching. In the Peak District the problems have been immense, and drastic measures are having to be introduced or considered. (See case study, page 15.) Similar problems have arisen in parts of the Yorkshire Dales, although efforts there to introduce traffic control schemes were dropped because of local opposition. On Dartmoor, traffic resulting from the 8 million annual visits has grown steadily in recent years, and could soon, the park authority has suggested, provoke severe restrictions if left to increase unchecked.[1]

Country congestion: are drastic measures now needed to control traffic in the national parks?

Country life

For those who live in the countryside, the arrival of tourists can be a mixed blessing. Many people in rural communities dislike change, especially if imposed on them by outside agencies. On the other hand, as they know better than anyone, and in stark contrast to the rural idyll assumed by outsiders, the countryside can be a difficult, frustrating and depressing place to live in. Although the population in rural areas is now rising again, the recent history is one of decades of decline in the quality of life. Agriculture has been severely diminished, bus services have deteriorated, village shops and schools have closed, and the younger generation has fled to the towns. Nearly 40% of parishes are without a shop; 60% have no primary school; 74% have no doctor; 22% are without mains sewerage. One in every five households is now thought to be living on or below the poverty line.[2] So any initiative that might help the local economy has to be considered.

In recent years there's been a growth in activity amongst tourist agencies and local authorities, which have identified tourism as a source for local employment – especially since foreign tourists are visiting the countryside in increasing numbers. So while traditional rural jobs have declined, those in tourism in rural areas have increased: according to government figures they now stand at 400,000. Much of the recent activity has involved encouraging and helping visitors to appreciate aspects of the countryside through the creation of new museums, historical trails, and other forms of interpretation.

Other threats

Other pressures for change that relate to tourism are also evident. For instance, the government has come under fire for its decision to review ownership of the large areas of woodland owned by the Forestry Commission. Every year 50 million recreational visits by walkers, campers, birdwatchers, joggers, picnickers and many others are made to these 2.8 million acres, some situated within the national parks. If all or part of this woodland is privatised, it's by no means certain that the right of access will remain. The resulting loss of recreational facilities would be enormous.

Access is also an issue in relation to the million acres owned by the Ministry of Defence and used for military training. The ministry claims that by generally forbidding public use of this land, it has preserved landscapes and hundreds of flora and fauna that would otherwise have been ruined by millions of trampling feet. This is a reasonable argument; as the cultural historian Patrick Wright recently put it: 'If you're a natterjack toad, the best place to be is on an army firing-range.'[3] The argument partly revolves around whether the army needs so much land, but mainly around access. This has been improved recently, but not enough for many countryside organisations. Some believe the military ought not to be on common land that should be open to everyone; others feel it should certainly not be active in the national parks – it has the use of nearly 15% of Dartmoor – where quiet enjoyment is meant to be given priority.

Demeaning the Past: The United States of America

The Disney Corporation recently announced plans to build a theme park in Haymarket, Virginia, which would offer a 'fun journey' through the history of the American Civil War period. The three thousand-acre site would contain 2,280 homes, 1,300 hotel rooms, shops, 1.9 million square feet of office space, and would offer animatronics, 'infotainment' and funfair rides for an expected five million visitors a year.

The scheme was controversial because the proposed location was close to the battlefield of Manassas, a centre for several civil war sites, including the first great battle of the war. It was also opposed on the grounds that it would trivialise America's history, and destroy a national park for ever.

The dispute was the subject of an investigation by a committee of inquiry in Washington, set up to decide how and where Americans should 'relate to their history'. Disney lost its case, and is now looking for an alternative site.

Cultural tourism

People have been visiting the country homes of writers, artists, musicians and others for many a decade. But the increasing popularity of such cultural tourism is creating the same kind of problem as other forms of tourism.

In the UK the problems are probably seen at their worst in the Lake

District. For example, in 1994 around 80,000 people visited Dove Cottage, the home of William and Dorothy Wordsworth just outside Grasmere: in August alone there were more than 14,000 visitors. There are even greater pressures at Hill Top, a tiny seventeenth-century farmhouse near Sawrey which was the former home of the writer Beatrix Potter, and which she left to the National Trust on her death. In the summer months as many as a thousand visitors a day come up in busloads from Ambleside, to be in the place where she wrote some of her famous children's books. The queue for entry can be lengthy and delays extensive; some visitors actually fail to get in. The National Trust is now considering ways in which it can control the numbers.

What chance is there of taking in the atmosphere of such places in such circumstances? This is one of the issues causing a dispute over facilities for visitors at Edward Elgar's birthplace in Worcestershire. Plans to build a visitor centre and a car park next to the cottage in Lower Broadheath in which he was born are being opposed, on the grounds that it would ruin the atmosphere Elgar wanted to preserve there. The protesters believe it would be more appropriate to create an Elgar Centre for English Music in nearby Malvern; the Elgar Foundation, which owns the site adjacent to the cottage, says the village atmosphere has already been spoilt, and that there should be room for both projects.

Conservation can also be a problematic issue in relation to literary haunts. Dorset County Council recently decided to restore Black Heath in Dorset, made famous by Thomas Hardy as Egdon Heath, to its original heathland state – it had become overgrown with vegetation. The heath stretches behind Hardy's cottage birthplace in Higher Bockhampton, which is owned by the National Trust, and is a key point on the literary trail for Hardy enthusiasts. The plan has had a mixed reception: some have praised the council for its decision to restore the heath to how it might have been in Hardy's day; others have accused it of trying to create a bogus authenticity, or of exhibiting a 'theme-park mentality'.

This part of Dorset has long been called 'Hardy Country'. Yet the explicit packaging of parts of the countryside linking them to celebrated popular writers seems to be getting out of hand, with South Shields becoming 'Catherine Cookson Country' and the Vale of York around

Thirsk now dubbed 'James Herriott Country'. The latter, of course, is as much to do with the television series based on his stories. But several tourist bodies are now selling the attractions of certain places principally on the basis of their use as locations for television series: recent examples include Holmfirth in the Pennines *(Last of the Summer Wine)*, Stamford .*(Middlemarch)* and Goathland in the North Yorkshire Moors *(Heartbeat)*. So now we have a new breed of cultural tourist, for whom the English, Scottish and Welsh tourist boards have helpfully produced a special map of 'Film and TV Locations in Britain'. The trend has produced its absurdities, such as when a crew filming *Heartbeat* had to look for a fresh location because of being constantly pestered by the very tourists the series had created.

In one way, this kind of cultural tourism is no different from that which relates to Hardy's Wessex or the Brontës' Moorland. Yet such promotions tend to offer visitors second-hand experience – a place is to be enjoyed because a scene was filmed there, rather than for its intrinsic value, or for the effect it had on an admired writer who responded to and captured the essential spirit of the place. They also tend to be mounted without consultation with local people, or without any consideration of the intrusion 'cultural tourists' can cause in their lives.

Golf War: Thailand

Thousands of peasant farming families have been turned off their land to make way for the increasing number of golf courses being built in south-east Asia to cater for tourists and others. As a result, Amnesty International has had to create a new category of 'golfing' prisoner of conscience.

In Thailand between 1989 and 1994, local developers created 160 courses, most of them out of rice fields in agricultural regions. Some are eighty times the size of a typical European course, and include luxury hotels, conference centres, fitness suites and even private airstrips.

Though the golf courses are supposed to be self-sufficient, it's claimed that they take water from reservoirs illegally, or dam up streams that flow through them towards the reservoir, so making present drought conditions worse.

Most caddies are women, some of whom are used by the players as prostitutes after the game.

Using the land

There have been many changes in the way the British countryside has been used in recent years. There appears to be a growing problem in some areas in balancing the enjoyment and use of the countryside with the preservation of its essential character. In 1994 the Council for the Protection of Rural England published *Leisure Landscapes*, a report which highlights the pressures being put on the countryside by the tourism and leisure industries. The authors show how new uses of the land, combined with changing public taste, are prompting a whole range of conflicts over how the countryside can or should be used, and creating a number of new cultural tensions as a result.

Many of these conflicts have arisen as a result of the growth in newer kinds of holiday or leisure attractions. One of the more controversial of these is the Center Parcs holiday village, the third of which opened in Wiltshire in the summer of 1994. (See case study, page 66.) Another that has aroused passions is the golf course. In England in 1992 no fewer than 1890 planning applications for building golf courses were lodged, and they are said already to take up 0.5% of the land.[4] Because they can have an adverse affect on the landscape and on nature conservation, as well as create new traffic problems, they have frequently been objected to at local level.

One of the points made by their critics is that the golf courses are often associated with other kinds of developments that come in their wake, such as hotels, new housing estates, or time-share accommodation. These may be totally inappropriate for their rural surroundings. Similar problems of visual intrusiveness can arise when old farm buildings are turned into leisure complexes or holiday homes.

One of the more recent controversies has been over the siting of windfarms, which appear to divide tourists and local people alike. The environmentally friendly turbines create a lot of anxiety about noise and visual intrusion before they are built, but tend to be more readily accepted afterwards. Indeed, the oldest windfarm in Britain, at Delabole in Cornwall, is now a tourist attraction in itself, complete with visitor centre, to which 100,000 people came during its first year.

Theme parks are another source of conflict, not least because they use up large tracts of land. There are now fifteen of these in the UK, with more likely to follow. The biggest is the 600-acre Alton Towers in Staffordshire, which can hold a staggering 25,000 people, 7,000 cars, and 400 coaches, and which was visited in 1992 by 2.5 million people. Traffic is of course a major issue with these parks; many are situated in the countryside, and not always accessible by public transport.

The growing use of the countryside for sports activities is also throwing up problems. Water sports may create levels of noise that are unacceptable to many people, as has happened with the coming of power boats to the Lake District (see page 11). The increasing popularity of other sports is also creating tensions between different groups using the same space. This has happened with traditional sports such as fishing and boating, where there have been clashes with those involved in canoeing.

A further source of conflict has been the mountain bike. There are now 5.5 million of these, and competitive mountain biking is the fastest growing UK sport. But conflicts have arisen, mainly with walkers and climbers, as to whether their two very different activities are compatible on the fells and mountainsides. With ownership predicted to increase, the problem is not going to go away in a hurry.

Even one of the older forms of recreation is creating certain problems. Horse-riding and pony-trekking are becoming increasingly popular in many places, including areas such as the North York Moors National Park. But they're now leading to a demand for equestrian centres and other new buildings, some of which can adversely affect the landscape. In addition, where there are not enough proper routes, there can be excessive wear and tear on the bridleways, making life difficult for walkers.[5]

It's within the context of all these different problems, which in the UK threaten the very future of parts of the countryside, that the need for alternative approaches to tourism is being gradually recognised, and serious consideration being given to the principles of sustainable tourism. But how realistic is it to expect us as tourists to behave in a different and more thoughtful way at precisely the moment when we may want to forget all our responsibilities? And how can those in the tourism business, who have generally shown scant regard up to now for the effect their operations have on the environment, be persuaded to change their ways?

A New Identity
The Tarka Project

The pace is about right: fast enough to let me relish the warm wind streaming against my face, slow enough to catch glimpses of the gorgeous green Devon countryside through gaps in the hedgerows. This, I decide, is the only way to travel. My hired mountain bike, yellow and mauve and bursting with gears, gives me a wonderful freedom to roam around this exquisite part of rural Devon. At one moment I'm riding smoothly along virtually empty country lanes around the village of Eggesford; the next I'm pedalling over the rugged paths of Flashdown Wood, matted with bluebells, and still steaming gently in the aftermath of the rain that fell earlier on this late spring morning.

But my pleasure is not due simply to the delights of nature. In the village of Wembworthy I stop at a delightful small stone church set back from the roadside. Its graveyard has the widest oak tree trunk I've ever seen. Inside there's a list of rectors for the parish, going back to Richard de Beresford's tenure in 1250. Further on, joining up again with the River Taw a couple of miles north of my starting-point, I cycle past the magnificent cedar, fir and pine standing in Heywood Wood. Here once stood a Norman castle, and the mound of its ramparts is still visible from the track.

The cycle route I've chosen is one of those recommended at the Eggesford Garden Centre, one of several points in the area where you can exchange four wheels for two for the day. Providing such a facility is just one small but important element in the Tarka Project, a tourism and conservation initiative with a growing national reputation, which aims at once to protect the character of this still unspoilt part of the West

Country, to encourage people to use it responsibly for recreation, and to preserve the unique wildlife of the area.

It was one man's passionate interest in a particular species of wildlife that provided the spur for the project to be set up in what is now known as 'Tarka Country'. For it was within this astonishingly varied landscape, encompassing Exmoor and Dartmoor at one extreme and the enclosed wooded valleys of the rivers Taw and Torridge at the other, that the writer Henry Williamson set his classic story *Tarka the Otter*.

Although the tale was first published in 1927, most of the countryside and the varied wildlife of the region described in it remain unchanged today. Williamson, who had been in the trenches throughout the First World War, came here in 1921, to escape the memories of the horrors of those years in France, to get away from his family, and to find somewhere more congenial to live than the London suburbs. The tiny Skirr Cottage in Georgeham near Woolacombe Sands on the north Devon coast became his home for many years.

Here he lived like a hermit, his door forever open to animals. Then one day he helped to save a young otter whose mother had been shot by a farmer, and made it part of his household. Later it escaped, and it was while he was searching for it amongst the otter haunts along the Taw and Torridge rivers flowing off Exmoor and Dartmoor that the idea of writing the work which eventually became *Tarka the Otter* first came to him.

The book, which won the Hawthornden Prize for Literature in 1928, has never been out of print since, and has been translated into several languages. Although the density of the description of nature and the dearth of human characters may make it difficult to read as a story, there's no doubting Williamson's power to evoke the spirit and feel of this part of the English countryside. His extraordinarily intimate knowledge of what he called 'The Country of the Two Rivers', and his obsession with describing it accurately, have given us an invaluable record of what the area was like some seventy years ago. And although he used invented place names, local people have had no difficulty in identifying the precise route of Tarka's journey up and down the Taw and Torridge rivers, round the coast of the Severn Sea from Lynton to the Estuary, or along Braunton Sands.

Cyclists follow the Tarka Trail across the Torridge Viaduct at Torrington, Devon.

Today this 180-mile route, known as the Tarka Trail, has become the centrepiece of the Tarka Project. Opened in the spring of 1992, and essentially a long-distance footpath, the trail forms a figure of eight centring on the medieval town of Barnstaple, and passes through many different types of landscape. Some thirty miles of it follow a former railway line, parts of which are now open to cyclists and horse riders. It includes rights of way such as footpaths, bridleways and tracks, as well as, occasionally, minor roads. Some paths have been specially created after consultation with landowners. The trail also passes through Exmoor and Dartmoor National Parks, land owned by the National Trust and the Forestry Commission, and a National Nature Reserve.

'I think the project has given the area an identity which it didn't have before,' says Beverley Trowbridge, the project's manager. 'People are using the name a lot, and becoming fond of it. And they're certainly making a lot of use of the Tarka Trail, which has been the lynchpin in the project.'

One of the key aims of the project has been to persuade you to leave your car behind when you enter Tarka Country. This is made easier by the existence of the Tarka Line, which runs for nearly 40 miles between Exeter and Barnstaple along the river valleys of the Yeo and the Taw. The journey along it is a delight, as the train moves at a stately pace past gentle hills, apple orchards, dense woods and isolated farms, the winding river always within sight, but frequently crossing beneath the railway line.

If you decide not to come by car, your life is made a great deal easier by a simple but invaluable service. Many local people offering accommodation – including the family in whose beautiful old farmhouse in Chawleigh I stayed overnight – are prepared to collect you from the nearest station on the line, and drop you off there at the end of your visit.

The project has done much to encourage travel on foot, whether you want to experience the wildness of the moorlands or the more varied charms of the gentler river valleys. It has produced *The Tarka Trail: A Walkers' Guide*, a book which includes detailed maps of different parts of the trail, with vivid route descriptions by Henry Williamson's son Richard. The leaflets which complement the book provide not only route details and points of interest along the way, but information on the nearest bus routes for each of the walks listed.

While walking is seen as an environmentally friendly way of exploring Tarka Country, cycling is also being heavily promoted. There are eight bicycle hire points within the region, where you can pick up information about the most suitable and interesting routes in the locality. The latest development is a two-year pilot scheme for a Bike Bus, which started operating in the Torridge valley in the summer of 1994. A converted bus with space for six bikes, it gives cyclists the opportunity to travel more widely than otherwise. If it proves successful, another bus will be introduced in the Taw valley.

This new scheme has been set up to try and ease some of the difficulties facing the car-free visitor. Bus services in parts of Tarka Country are infrequent. There are also problems about taking bicycles on the Tarka Line. At present only one bike is allowed per carriage, a ruling which is causing the project team a great deal of anguish, as they try to get Regional Railways to be more flexible. 'It's a huge embarrassment to us when we're trying to encourage car-users to change their ways and use bicycles instead,' says Beverley Trowbridge. 'The railway company offers crazy reasons for not changing their policy, such as they haven't got the rolling stock. But I don't think they're looking for a solution; I think they're just coming up with obstacles.'

Encouraging the use of public transport is also one of the main aims of a separate body that has been set up through the project, the Tarka Country Tourist Association. Its membership, now numbering 140, consists of a range of small businesses that cater for tourists, mostly offering accommodation in farmhouses, guest houses and small hotels. In order to qualify, members have to sign a 'green charter' that commits them to work for the conservation of the area's character by asking them to make the following pledges:

- 'We will strive to ensure that as far as possible our activities have minimal impact on the environment, and in particular:
- We will endeavour to use environmentally friendly products and services, recycle waste where possible, and conserve energy.
- We will promote to visitors activities such as walking, cycling and horse riding, and encourage them to respect the life and work of the countryside during their visit.
- We will provide information for visitors on the wildlife and natural beauty of Tarka Country, and will encourage them to respect the life and work of the countryside during their visit.
- We will manage our grounds so as to maximise their wildlife and landscape potential, and will seek to ensure that our buildings contribute to, rather than detract from, the character of the locality.
- We will actively support conservation in Tarka Country.
- We will favour local products where possible.'

Chrissie Stevens, secretary of the association, is keen to emphasise that the charter is not meant to be a series of rules. 'We don't expect people to do everything straight away, but to see the items as things to be aimed at,' she says. 'The basic idea is to try and help people with small businesses to put sustainable tourism into practice.'

The association has set up a number of different ventures. It has published a *Green Guide*, which includes useful information on different parts of Tarka Country, as well as a complete list of members of the association, and details of their charges for accommodation. Its most recent venture is the formation of a group of local producers, who have put together a leaflet giving details of their produce, and where it can be bought.

Conservation has from the start been at the heart of the Tarka Project, and raising additional funds for it is also seen as one of the association's aims. At present they are looking at potential ways of raising such money from visitors. One scheme being piloted is a voluntary levy of 50p on accommodation bills, or a few extra pence on meals provided or produce sold.

Another scheme already in existence is the Friends of Tarka. All the money raised through this body will be used for conservation projects involving work such as riverbank and woodland management, pond creation and otter surveys. So far money has been used to re-plant one of the riverside trees near Tarka's birthplace at Beam Bridge, Torrington. And for the forthcoming centenary of Henry Williamson's birth, funds will be used to re-plant an area around his old writing hut, where the original trees were planted by the writer himself.

If Tarka's creator were somehow able to return to this lovely part of Devon, he'd no doubt be astonished to find his otter's name attached to a tourism initiative. But he'd surely approve of a project which seems to be having some considerable success in protecting the landscape which meant so much to him.

4 Obstacles to Change

'How many hellholes are we prepared to create on the way to paradise?'

Jonathon Porritt[1]

It is clear that sustainable tourism will only have a minimal impact if it remains an idea embraced by a minority of people. No substantial progress will be made unless the idea permeates the places and the manner in which most of us take holidays or enjoy the countryside. Ecotourism may be growing in popularity, but it still only takes around 5% of the holiday market. Demand for the traditional kind of holiday is not going to slacken in the immediate future. Nor are people suddenly going to stop visiting the honeypot areas in the countryside or at historic sites. Unless the issue of mass tourism is tackled head-on, sustainable tourism will simply be a pipe dream.

There are of course huge obstacles to be overcome, even leaving aside the predicted growth in tourism for the rest of the century. Some of the most formidable relate to the mass holiday market. They include people's traditional attitudes to what holidays are about; the rigidly commercial aims of the tour operators; and the failure of developers and local politicians to see beyond the short term. More generally, there's the difficulty of persuading tourism businesses that sustainability can be profitable as well as environmentally responsible; and the reluctance of governments to match their rhetoric on the subject of tourism with adequate funding.

Public attitudes

Perhaps the most intractable problem is that of traditional attitudes to going on holiday. Generally speaking, it's a time when most of us want to just switch off our normal lives, and tune in to a lifestyle that is totally different, whether it involves sun, sea, sport, adventure, culture or romance.

Alison Stancliffe, a founder member of Tourism Concern, a body advocating just and sustainable tourism, is one of many who sees this as a major problem: 'For most people, the essence of holidays is escape,' she says. 'The very act of going on holiday involves closing your eyes to things you might normally care about. At such times people just want to shut off from issues such as conservation, rather than look them in the face.'[2]

Tour operators sometimes take up this point to justify a refusal to change their normal practices. If people really want a more sustainable kind of tourism, they argue, we would of course provide it. Hugh Somerville, who works in the environmental branch of British Airways, says: 'To be cynical, the main problem is human nature. At one end of the spectrum you have the sun-seeker and the lager lout, at the other the ecotourist. There's certainly a pull towards ecotourism, but it's difficult to shift human awareness. The distribution is skewed towards the unthinking end of the market. It's not going to be a revolution; it has to be a gradual process.'[3]

According to Andrew Blaza, director of the World Travel and Tourism Council Environment Research Centre, there's little evidence of people's willingness to change. 'There's virtually no information to be had about the public's attitudes,' he says. 'Most of what there is is anecdotal and comes from tour operators, who say customers don't want to make purchasing decisions about holidays based on green principles.'[4]

There have been some opinion surveys on the subject. Recent research by the World Tourism Organisation showed that 85% of German tourists say they want a holiday that is 'environmentally correct'. A survey in the US revealed that 40% of American tourists were interested in what was called 'life-enhancing' as opposed to 'sun-seeking' travel. But what people say to a researcher and what they actually do may be very different. John Elkington, director of Sustainability, uncovered some depressing facts from tour operators while researching the book he wrote with Julia Hailes, *Holidays That Don't Cost the Earth*. 'We talked to One World Tours, and their response was that it was one thing for the consumers to buy a green detergent, quite another to buy a green holiday,' he recalls. 'But I was particularly struck by the reaction of Cox and King's. They said that they had seen a growth in the numbers of people buying wildlife holidays, but no real evidence of deep-seated environmental awareness. And, equally interesting, they had had no real feedback on their offer to buy, and thereby conserve, an acre of rain-forest for every booking made.' [5]

The situation varies of course from country to country. It's reckoned that some 20% of tourists from Germany and Switzerland can be classified as 'ecologically critical' consumers. There's some feeling that the British are more entrenched in their attitudes than people in many other countries. Martin Brackenbury, chairman of the Federation of Tour Operators, is one who takes this view: 'There are huge numbers of people totally indifferent to the idea of sustainable tourism, especially in the UK. Despite the work of people like Attenborough and Bellamy, we're not so familiar with the idea in this country. It hasn't really made any difference to the great unwashed. A lot of people muck up their own back yard, and do just the same on holiday. There's much greater awareness of such issues in Germany, Austria and Switzerland.' [6]

The tour operators

There's no doubt that tour operators have in the past been as much to blame as anyone for the enormous amount of damage caused by mass tourism. The promotion and selling of the package holiday, based on a cynical and exploitative 'boom-and-bust' philosophy, has effectively ruined the physical and cultural landscape of many regions around the world. As Martin Brackenbury puts it: 'There are down-market operators who don't bother about the environment at all.' [7]

The destruction has been caused in part by the intense competitiveness amongst tour companies. In the UK, for instance, there are over six hundred operators, and an astonishing 20,000 organisations of varying sizes putting together holiday packages. The pressure on companies to increase their profits and share of the market is intense – which is one reason why they're always looking for new destinations to exploit, with little care for the consequences.

Profit margins are minuscule when calculated per person – 50p a flight is one current estimate – so numbers are absolutely crucial. This means that the over-riding motivation for some companies is to fill their aircraft. Yet the problem for tour operators is that moves towards sustainable tourism will involve a restriction on numbers, both at the destination and on flights. This is anathema to them, since it will be seen to have an adverse effect on their profits.

Because of such commercial demands, problems tend to multiply when a destination becomes popular, and operators start putting heavy pressure on the local tourist trade to expand their facilities. Noel Josephides, chairman of the Association of International Tour Operators, has described succinctly the process that can so often follow when a destination becomes flavour of the month:

'We begin financing more building, even if the host country is pulling back on finance; the fact is, we feel there is a demand, the local hoteliers want money, and we have got the money. We know there is going to be volume, so we begin to finance building. And generally at this stage, and this is a very important stage, the host country is overwhelmed by the fact that it is popular. And it misses the first signs of a problem that is to come. What happens is that because it is popular, then there is too much capacity. Because there is too much capacity, it has to be discounted, and discounting leads to the fact that no one makes any money. At this stage the hoteliers step in and generally put up prices, because they feel that everything is going very well, this flow will never stop, and so why not make a bit of a killing on it first? So up go the prices, and inevitably the demand falls.' [8]

The short-term view

It's this familiar sequence of events that can lead to particular destinations being suddenly drastically under-booked one year, after having been hugely popular in the previous one. The pattern has been repeated in many places, leaving resorts and their newly-built accommodation half empty, as the operators move on to different destinations.

This sudden shift in the popularity of a destination is hardly surprising.

The 'get-rich-quick' mentality of the tour operators, and of developers and hoteliers – often themselves local people with entrepreneurial ambitions – has resulted in the construction of a mass of low-quality, visually hideous buildings. Not only are they thoroughly unattractive in themselves, they also manage to deprive the place of the very qualities that attracted tourists there in the first place. So those who want quality and local distinctiveness on their holidays look elsewhere, and the place quickly loses its broad appeal. Once a destination gets into this cycle, it becomes difficult to reverse it. Unused and uncared-for buildings start to deteriorate, and many resorts end up becoming down-market ghettoes, almost indistinguishable from each other.

Benidorm in Spain. Uncontrolled and inappropriate development has blighted hundreds of tourist resorts in Europe.

This pattern has been repeating itself for many years in many different parts of the world. Yet there is little sign that any real lessons have been learned. Uncontrolled development, assisted in many places by widespread corruption, continues to blot the landscape of previously unspoilt areas, and to ruin the distinctive environments of a huge number of places. Will we have to run out of destinations to spoil before a halt is called to the destruction?

Most tour operators still seem reluctant to change their practice. In 1992 the environmental body Ark mounted a campaign to persuade tourists to face up to their environmental responsibilities. Believing information to be an important strand of the campaign, they tried to interest several tour operators in the idea of including information about local culture in their brochures. Roisin Orosz, Ark's campaigns director, remembers the reaction: 'We went round all the big tour operators, but none was interested,' she says. 'They said they were worried about alarming or browbeating tourists, that it would seem goody-goody. But I think a lot of it is lack of will: if they had the resolve to do it, they would.'

Business sense

The prime aim of most businesses is to make money for all those who have a stake in them. This is as much the case within the tourism industry as in any other. So it's not surprising that attempts to persuade businesses to think of their environmental responsibilities have generally fallen on stony ground. This is despite the fact that many national environmental bodies and local tourism initiatives have tried to show that, by adopting a policy that takes environmental issues seriously, businesses will prosper in the long run – not least because many of their customers are becoming more demanding about standards of environmental care.

Convincing businesses of this argument is proving an uphill struggle, as is acknowledged in the booklet *The Green Light: A Guide to Sustainable Tourism*, published by the English Tourist Board in 1992, in which the benefits are spelt out. 'Many tourism businesses, large and small, are currently foregoing the benefits of going green because they don't appreciate the value of a green policy,' it says. Nevertheless, a minority of businesses are now beginning to heed this kind of advice, and changing their practice accordingly. (See page 115.)

Controlling the Numbers: Galapagos Islands, Ecuador

There are 13 main islands in the Galapagos archipelago, with a population of around 4,500. Thirty years ago fewer than 20 visitors a week visited the islands, the home of the celebrated Galapagos tortoises and other rare species of wildlife.

Today the islands are attracting 'ecotourists' in their thousands. The Ecuador government decided to set a 'sustainable limit' to such visitors of 12,000 a year, but for economic reasons then raised the figure to 50,000 a year. It's believed that thousands more come in illegally by boat, to avoid the substantial entrance tax. Many come in order to make money out of tourists, and are the cause of much of the unmanaged development that is endangering the islands' wildlife.

The tourists earn $50 million a year for Ecaudor, but little of the money goes back to the islanders. Hotel development has resulted in pollution, and many natural habitats are being destroyed in what used to be one of the most protected areas in the world.

Government action

Governments have often been slow to come round to the idea of sustainable tourism. Only in the last few years, as concern about environmental matters has become more widespread amongst the public, and the situation has begun to reach crisis point in certain areas, have they begun to take any serious action.

The report of the UK government's task force *Maintaining the Balance*, published in 1991, was certainly a step in the right direction (see page 26). Yet while a broad welcome was given to the report's acknowledgement of the importance of sustainable tourism, it was deficient in a number of respects.

One was that the special problems relating to seaside resorts and coastal areas were not considered. Another was that no guidance was given to tourism businesses as to how they could improve their environmental performance and yet remain profitable – although this omission was partially rectified by the publication the following year of the *Green Light* booklet. Finally, the task force left out of its definition of sustainable tourism the crucially important role of the tourism industry itself.

Some conservationists questioned the underlying assumptions the report made about balance. One of these was Paul Gompertz, director of the Devon Wildlife Trust. 'We must not allow ourselves to take for granted that tourism is entering an already balanced equation between man and his environment,' he said. After citing the failure of many West Country beaches to meet European bathing standards, the loss of wildlife habitats, and the poor quality of rivers in the region, he added: 'This is the status quo upon which the stresses of additional tourism might be imposed. Is this the balance we are seeking to maintain?' [9]

The report failed to recommend that the government should make up the significant shortfall in funding needed for tourism, suggesting instead that the money should be provided either by the industry or by the visitor. Bernard Lane, director of the Rural Tourism Development Project at the University of Bristol, was one of many who believed this to be misguided: 'The government represents the community,' he argued. 'The community benefits from environmentally responsible tourism. It benefits both from a better environment and from the wider social and economic benefits which a successful tourism industry brings. Therefore the public purse should help to pay. Only the government can coordinate and give long-term cohesion to environmental initiatives.' [10]

Although the report may have helped to raise the consciousness of many politicians, this hasn't been translated into concrete action. As one leading figure in the field puts it: 'Five years ago, whenever I talked to ministers about the subject, they would never have mentioned sustainable tourism. Now they all talk about it all the time. But mostly there is more talk than action. There's much more awareness, but it's a highly politically charged subject.' [11]

However, in the years since *Maintaining the Balance* appeared, the UK government has continued to see its role as mainly an enabling one. In general it has adopted a hands-off approach, believing the matter should be left to the private sector working in partnership with the main tourist agencies. For some in the tourism field, this suggests the momentum created by the task force has been lost. Richard Denman, a tourism consultant, says: 'The government has forgotten some of the things it was talking about four years ago. Time has moved on, and I'm not sure it has sustained its interest in the issue.'[12]

The point is reinforced by the way responsibility for tourism has changed within the government, and the fact that tourism and the environment are located in different departments. Until shortly after the setting up of the task force it was looked after by the Department of Employment. As a result, most of the emphasis had been on creating and maintaining jobs in the tourist industry. But in the spring of 1991 tourism was made the responsibility of the newly created Department of National Heritage (DNH), though almost as an afterthought. Yet far from giving it a stronger profile, this move appears to have had the opposite effect in the succeeding years. Neil Sinden, heritage campaigner for the Council for the Protection of Rural England, is one of many who are critical of its performance: 'The DNH appears to be overwhelmingly concerned with the short-term, commercial potential of the industry, with the environment taking a back seat. It is vital that the department adopts a new approach to its tourism responsibilities, which gives greater recognition to the fundamental importance of the quality of the environment to the long-term success of the tourist industry.'[13]

Such a view is supported by the government's subsequent attitude to funding tourism initiatives. During the 1980s several Tourism Development Action Programmes (TDAPs) had been funded through the English Tourist Board (ETB), the regional tourist boards, and other agencies. In the wake of the task force report, the government encouraged the ETB and the regional tourist boards to set up several pilot projects. These were to tackle the issue of visitor management in areas such as the Peak District, the Surrey Hills, Stratford-upon-Avon, the Lake District and South Devon. By the end of 1994 these projects had either come to the end of their life, or were about to do so.

Meanwhile the government had drastically reduced the funding of the ETB and, to a lesser extent, that of the regional tourist boards. In 1992

Peter Brooke, then Secretary of State at the Department of National Heritage, wrote to the ETB, saying that tourism was now a 'mature industry' and no longer needed government help. Its position was unchanged two years later: 'Through the ETB's pioneering work the tourism industry now has a far greater appreciation of how its future relies on the quality of our environment,' a DNH spokesman stated. 'Accordingly, the government feels that it is now for the industry to take forward this work, and maintain this country's reputation as a front runner in the field of sustainable tourism.' [14]

However, at the ETB the number of staff was reduced from 130 to 55 over those two years. The result has been a drastic reduction in the amount of development and environmental work undertaken. Stephen Mills, the ETB's assistant director of development, says it's no longer clear whether the government is interested in encouraging good practice: 'We used to be seen as the leading tourist board in Europe,' he says. 'Now we can no longer claim to be that. I don't know what the government is playing at. They say it's up to others to take things forward, but who is that going to be? We're being asked to be more of a strategic body, but we haven't the cash to do anything. It's a crazy situation.' [15]

Sex Tourism: South-East Asia

In countries such as Thailand, Sri Lanka and the Philippines, the substantial increase in child prostitution is directly related to the rise of tourism, which has created a trade that involves hundreds of thousands of children.

Except for a small female market in the Philippines, sex-tourists in the region are exclusively male. Most come from Japan, Australia, America and Western Europe, with England supplying the most European tourists in this category.

The Campaign to End Child Prostitution in Asian Tourism (ECPAT) is working for changes in the law in individual countries, to give children greater protection. Its director Ron O'Grady said: 'The demand of western tourists is increasing the number of children in prostitution to disproportionately high figures. The situation must be dealt with internationally.'

The impression is now widespread that, despite government statements, tourism has become a peripheral concern, and the development work of the tourism agencies given a much lower priority. Some critics believe the tourist boards have become little more than trade associations, and that without wider representation of environmental and local community interests, the impact of tourism will never be effectively controlled.

Kerry Godfrey, lecturer in tourism development at Oxford Brookes University, is one of the sceptics: 'The key problem is lack of political will,' he suggests. 'The only policy is set out in the Tourism Planning Policy Guidance Note, and that doesn't say anything; indeed I think it sets out the opposite of support for tourism. Meanwhile the tourist boards have become little more than marketing bureaux, so doing development work is difficult. They don't do sustainable development, they do industry development.' [16]

Given all these obstacles, the possibility of fundamental change must seem unlikely. Yet both in the UK and elsewhere, many groups and organisations are trying to promote and encourage a more sustainable approach to tourism. In the second half of this book I look in some detail at what they are doing – not just in England, but in Wales, Scotland, Northern Ireland and the Republic of Ireland, all countries facing great challenges in trying to encourage and support sustainable tourism.

Paradise Invented

The Holiday Village

As we wander through the forest in the June sunshine, I catch a
glimpse of a chalet through the trees and ask Barry Collins about it.
He smiles wryly as he corrects my mistake. 'Actually we call them villas
here. Chalets are for Butlins.'

Sherwood Forest Holiday Village, created in 1987 on 400 acres of
Robin Hood country near Nottingham, certainly seems to offer a very
different experience to that of a traditional holiday camp. For a start it's a
village, not a camp, and it has guests, not campers. Secondly, one of the
main claims made by the holiday company Center Parcs for its purpose-
built, traffic-free village is that it offers you a holiday that combines
privacy with a chance to get 'in close touch with nature'. Hence the
'villas' – which are actually low, single-storey stone buildings with large
windows, situated among the conifers and gorse bushes in the wooded
areas of the village.

Great care appears to have been lavished on the natural environment
at Sherwood. Barry Collins is the grounds maintenance manager, and an
obvious enthusiast for conservation. 'I get to play with nature,' he
observes, as we walk on through his woodland kingdom. We pause on a
bridge that crosses a stream, which he tells me has in it 25 species of
water vegetation. He talks proudly of the wildlife that lives in the forest:
'We create a habitat, and along comes the animal,' he explains.
Kingfisher, heron, tawny owls, woodpeckers, nightjars and eleven species
of dragonfly can all be found here, as can rabbits, squirrels, and fallow
deer.

Holiday villages are a relatively recent phenomenon in the UK, but are well established in Holland, where they originated in the late 1960s. The idea was based on what the Dutch call *tussendoor* – a short break taken when needed at any time of the year. With facilities which include an indoor swimming area complete with subtropical temperatures, the villages were able to provide an 'all-season' holiday, minimising the effect of poor weather on people's enjoyment. The idea caught on and Center Parcs now operates seven villages in Holland, as well as two in Belgium, two in France, and one to open soon in Germany.

Britain, with its famously unpredictable weather, must have seemed an obvious target for further development. Sherwood was in fact the first holiday village to be built in the UK, in 1987. Since then Center Parcs has created two more. The second, Elveden Forest, was built on Lord Iveagh's estate in the Brecklands, on the borders of Suffolk and Cambridgeshire. The third, which opened in the summer of 1994, is situated in Aucombe Wood on the 10,000-acre estate at Longleat in Wiltshire. Meanwhile Granada/Laing, trading under the name of Lakewoods, has gained planning permission to create three villages: one near Market Weighton in Humberside, one in Somerford Keynes near Cirencester, and one in Whinfell Forest in Cumbria.

There's no doubt that sites are chosen carefully. Center Parcs opts for existing forest areas so that the villages can be easily screened from the surrounding countryside, both during construction and afterwards. It selects sites which are of relatively low ecological value, where there may be few indigenous plants and animals, but which are capable of being enhanced by the creation of new types of habitat. At the planning stage efforts are made to keep the visual impact on the countryside to a minimum, while a planning appraisal aims to ensure that there are no adverse effects on the existing roads or on nearby towns and villages. Once preliminary plans are ready consultation with local people is arranged, by means of public meetings and exhibitions of the proposals.

Despite this very detailed planning, the introduction of this kind of holiday development on their doorsteps has sometimes brought mixed reactions. While some local people have supported the venture, opponents have been worried. Many of their worries have been about the noise and disturbance likely to be generated by traffic – Sherwood has space for 1,200 cars at any one time – although these fears seem to lessen once the village is actually operating. But local and national environmental and countryside organisations have also been divided: while many have supported the scheme, it has been argued that such developments are just not appropriate in certain kinds of rural settings, and are likely to be detrimental to the essential character of the countryside. There are also concerns that this kind of enterprise can make unacceptable demands on local physical resources and infrastructures.

The siting of the most recent Center Parcs village has also drawn criticism. The vast Longleat estate is owned by the Marquess of Bath, whose father was one of the first landowners after the Second World War to open up a great country house and its gardens to the public. Its appeal was enhanced for many visitors by the lions that used to wander around the estate. But its early popularity waned, and in the early 1990s agreement was reached with Center Parcs to lease the company a 400-acre commercial plantation on the estate. Here it would build a new holiday village catering for up to a quarter of a million visitors a year.

The conflict arose because the chosen site of Aucombe Wood was just inside Cranborne Chase and the West Wiltshire Downs, one of the Countryside Commission's designated Areas of Outstanding Natural Beauty (AONB). The scheme was therefore subject to planning restrictions designed to protect such areas. Essentially these mean that there can be no major development within an AONB unless it can be shown that it is in the national interest, and that no other site is available.

Although the Longleat scheme was supported by both the district and the county councils in Wiltshire, a public inquiry was called because the site was in an AONB. The inquiry inspector recommended that the development should go ahead, and the government granted planning permission in the summer of 1992. Two years later the village was open for business.

The Countryside Commission has said that the decision 'should not be seen as an indication that designated countryside is the right place' for such developments. Despite this, and reassurances from the government, there have been worries that the decision could create a dangerous precedent in relation to development in AONBs. A spokesman for the

Council for the Protection of Rural England (CPRE) said that the decision 'flatly contradicts government policies for protecting this outstandingly beautiful countryside, and opens the door to the tourist industry to ride roughshod over the planning system.' However, CPRE decided not to challenge the decision in the courts, even though preliminary legal advice seemed to suggest there was a reasonable chance of success if it did so.

The Countryside Commission, which is responsible for designating and managing AONBs, decided not to oppose the plan. It judged that the village would be unlikely fundamentally to alter the character of the landscape of the area, because the site could be well screened; and that the planting of new trees would be of benefit to the woodland, both visually and in terms of better management. It was impressed by the environmental record of Center Parcs, and felt that an exception should be made to the normal planning policy for AONB developments in this particular case.

For its part the government was persuaded by the fact that Longleat was already heavily used for recreational purposes, and by Center Parcs' plans for managing the traffic. It was also convinced that the proposed creation of 750 jobs was in the national interest.

Center Parcs makes a point of emphasising how the creation of its villages not only helps the employment situation locally, but also provides support for the local economy. Independent research has calculated that the value of business brought into an area, as the result of new jobs, additional purchasing for the needs of the village, and an increase in the number of visitors, can be valued at around £12.75 million per annum.

At Sherwood some 800 jobs have been created in order to meet the needs of the village's customers. Some work in the shops, restaurants and bars that are dotted around the village square; others help to run the many sports facilities, both indoors and out; others are employed to make sure the village runs efficiently, or to maintain and improve the environmental quality of the site.

After we had finished our tour of the grounds, Barry Collins took me into the 'Subtropical Swimming Paradise'. This is a large building with a plastic dome, which is kept at a constant temperature of 84 degrees all the year round. In it is a large swimming pool, surrounded by palm and other tropical trees – oranges and bananas apparently thrive here.

The Center Parcs brochure makes it clear what is being sold. Under the headline 'A Touch of the South Seas' it says: 'Here, in a balmy climate of 84 degrees, tropical vegetation thrives, creating an exotic environment that is close to fantasy. Spilling over with excitement, brimming with activity, it's a heady and intoxicating world. So bask in the illusion of a tropical cove, endlessly sunny by day and a wonder by night: a world of contrasts, where you can gasp in a cold plunge pool or sigh in the bliss of a warm whirlpool bath.... It's a masterpiece, a water creation unmatched anywhere.'

Today, in the middle of summer, the pool and its surrounds are packed full of families and couples on holiday, noisily making use of the slides and waves machines, some of them swimming directly into an outside pool in which guests apparently happily cavort in winter – even when it's snowing.

It was this scene that brought to the front of my mind a question that had been preoccupying me ever since I entered the village: how different are holiday villages from holiday camps? Center Parcs says its customers are principally 'ABC1 families who pay a little more to get what they want'. In other words, they're mainly a middle-class clientele, as opposed to the working-class one that the holiday camps cater for. There is a decided difference in style – as indicated by some of the more upmarket facilities such as the Country Club and Aqua Sana, the holistic health and beauty centre – but I was left with the feeling that what both kinds of companies are offering is a somewhat uniform holiday experience, in which it matters little whether, in the case of the holiday villages, you are in Suffolk, Nottinghamshire or Wiltshire.

Center Parcs clearly takes a responsible attitude towards the environment of its villages, and monitors its development meticulously. Yet there is still something a little odd in the claim that as a visitor you are getting 'in touch with nature', when you are actually surrounded by three thousand fellow holiday-makers living in seven hundred villas, and when, however spacious the grounds may be, you are fenced in and cut off from the world outside.

Center Parcs claims that this is what people want, and its record shows that it's right. A major attraction is the capacity of the domed building to be proof against the British weather. Occupancy rates are 90-95% on average all the year round, and 60% of visitors make repeat bookings. Vandalism is almost non-existent: youngsters are apparently too busy with all the activities on offer.

By gathering large numbers of holiday-makers together in a limited space within easy access of their homes, Center Parcs is certainly taking pressure off other areas, reducing energy costs, and so meeting some of the goals of sustainable tourism. Yet I find it hard to keep down an instinctive feeling that the creation by a large international company of such 'fantasy' holiday playgrounds in the middle of the English countryside, which bear no relation to the particular natural or cultural characteristics of rural life in the surrounding area, has to be an unwelcome development, and is ultimately not what sustainable tourism is about.

Yet the holiday village idea appears to be here to stay and Center Parcs is not the only player in the game. Lakewoods has not ruled out increasing its number of holiday villages. Another company, Sun Parks International, took an option under the name of Palm Resorts International on a site near Weston-super-Mare. And Rank has put in a planning application to build its first holiday village in Lyminge Forest in Kent.

There is also the possibility of the idea spreading into other parts of the UK. Yet another company, Leading Leisure, has recently taken a look at a site at Hoddom Castle near Lockerbie, in Dumfries and Galloway. The result could be the creation of a 'tropical paradise' catering for three thousand people amidst the subtle landscape of the Scottish lowlands.

5 Limiting the Damage

'Of all noxious animals, the most noxious is a tourist; and of all tourists, the most vulgar, ill-bred, offensive and loathsome is the British tourist.'

Reverend Francis Kilvert, *Diary*, 1870

At its worst, tourism has had an adverse and sometimes disastrous impact on some of our most cherished places. What efforts are being made to try to deal with these immense problems, and to persuade all the players in the game to take on board the principles of sustainable tourism?

Tourist behaviour

Changing the way we behave as tourists is no easy matter. Old habits die hard, and many of us are not interested in any idea which might appear to interfere with our having a Good Time, or restrict our freedom to go where we want, when we want. Yet many of us are prepared at least to think twice about the effect our actions as tourists may have on the environment, on local people, and on our own capacity to enjoy our holiday or visit.

One of the keys to change is education. This was one of the main elements in The Green Travel Bug Campaign mounted in 1992 by the environmental body Ark, in an attempt to influence the thinking and behaviour of British tourists visiting popular Mediterranean tourist resorts. 'The psychology of mass tourism is very interesting,' says Roisin Orosz, Ark's campaigns director. 'People stick together in ghettoes, partly fuelled by the fear of differences, so it becomes Them and Us. If you can show and explain to them the human side of the places they're going to, however simply, it can make a difference.'[1]

Ark's method was to produce a magazine called *Going For It: The Ark Guide to Sun, Sea, Sand and Saving the World!* Written in a breezy, popular style, it touched on some of the negative impacts of tourism. It drew attention, for instance, to the cruel treatment of animals used as tourist attractions on Spanish beaches; and to the need to avoid buying souvenirs such as coral, ivory bangles, shells and hardwood ornaments, which depend on the exploitation of wildlife or their habitats.

But it also suggested ways in which tourists could protect the natural environment of the country they were visiting 'and still have fun'. The essence of these ideas was incorporated into a Good Traveller Code. The magazine was distributed free at Manchester Airport, and an accompanying video was shown inflight on all Britannia Airways charter flights, reaching around 3 million holiday-makers a year.

Many tourism agencies and project teams are now producing codes of conduct to try to influence visitors' behaviour. The Countryside Commission has already done this with its Country Code, which has been adopted or adapted by some of the national parks. The code urges the public to respect the life and work of the countryside, to protect its wildlife, plants and trees, to help keep water clean, to take all litter home, and generally to behave in a sensible and thoughtful manner towards the landscape and the people who live there.

Unfortunately not everyone listens to such advice. Vandalism has been a problem in certain places, graffiti on Stonehenge being the most notorious example. Litter too is often a headache, and can sometimes be dangerous for animals. Some novel solutions have been found to deal with this problem. One was the idea dreamed up by the National Trust for the site of the fantastic rock formations at Brimham Rocks near Harrogate, near the Yorkshire Dales National Park. The 120,000 annual visitors were leaving a lot of litter, so the trust decided to remove all the bins, and provide visitors with bags in which to collect the litter. The result was a pristine landscape.[2]

The need for interpretation

Interpretation is widely seen as a good means of encouraging tourists to be more interested in the places they visit, in the hope that they will then take better care of them. It should not of course be confused with marketing or publicity, or the mere provision of factual information. One of the pioneers of interpretation, Freeman Tilden, usefully defined it in his book *Interpreting Our Heritage* as 'an educational activity which aims to reveal meanings and relationships through the use of original objects, by first-hand experience and by illustrative media'. How then can interpretation work best in relation to the goals of sustainable tourism?

One of the mottoes of the United States' National Park Service runs: 'Through interpretation, understanding; through understanding, appreciation; through appreciation, protection.' The idea that if you get to understand a place better you are more likely to value it would seem to be common sense. Whether that understanding is best gained by means of formal interpretation, and whether it subsequently leads to a desire to protect the place, are more complicated questions.

Different places invite different kinds of interpretation. In recent years, with the growth of visitor centres, one use for it has been as a means of controlling numbers. At Clovelly in Devon, for instance, a visitor centre has lessened the amount of intrusion experienced by residents, now that the story of the village is available to the 400,000 visitors who turn up every year. At Stonehenge, the new plans assume most visitors will be happy to see the stones from a distance and rely on the interpretation in the visitor centre, rather than take a two-mile walk to the circle itself (see page 76).

Yet the latter, happily, is an exceptional case. In general, the best kind of interpretation is surely that which allows you first-hand experience of the place you are visiting, perhaps with an experienced guide on hand to answer your questions. But this raises one of the key questions about interpretation: when does it become intrusive? At some times in some places, the last thing you may want is somebody telling you all about the fascinating history of the area. Printed information also has its drawbacks: it can be too solemn, too wordy or too quaint. It can also be highly selective in its content, perhaps reflecting only one view of the history of a place. Such a problem can easily arise in countries or regions where political divisions are sharpest, such as Northern Ireland.

Another issue is the tone and level of the interpretation. Tourists have not signed up for an evening class, and since their visit is likely to be a fleeting one, the touch needs to be kept light. As Bernard Lane says, in a useful essay on the potential and pitfalls of interpretation: 'It is very easy to interpret for the educated and motivated elite. It is, however, vital that the difficult task of interpretation for the mass audience with little time or interest must be tackled.'[3] On the other hand, although visitors may have come to a place for purely recreational purposes, they may end up having a thoroughly educational experience. Or, as Freeman Tilden puts it: 'He (sic) may be there for the explicit hope that you will reveal to him why he is there.'

Physical damage

The problem of physical damage inevitably tends to be at its most acute in the most popular spots, and at certain times of the year, usually during the summer months. The UK government's task force suggested the problems were not yet chronic or widespread, but that there was no room for complacency. In *Maintaining the Balance* it said: 'Some heritage sites and areas of countryside are being seriously damaged, and in a few places the problems are barely being contained. Some communities suffer as a result. In other places the impact of visitor pressure is cumulative, so that even modest levels of use can, after a number of years, provide a threat to the environment.'[4]

Stonehenge in Wiltshire is a symbol of many things to many people, but its present condition also symbolises the problems of damage caused by visitor pressure. Part of a World Heritage Site, and the most visited ancient monument in England, in 1993/94 it attracted 672,000 people through the turnstiles. The previous year it was estimated that a further 150,000 used the visitor facilities, but chose to view the celebrated prehistoric stones from the roadside.

Until 1978 the public was free to walk within the stone circle. But its increasing presence caused heavy erosion, making the grass bare, and exposing chalk that contained many archaeological remains. So the area was roped off. Since then, nylon mesh grids or 'plastic grass' have been used to reinforce the grass area and reduce erosion. In the meantime, the site had become popular for the celebration of the summer solstice, the number of visitors for the event rising to 30,000 by 1984. A ticket system was introduced; but when in 1989 large numbers of New Age

Travellers and others boycotted the system and walked to the site, there was a violent confrontation with the police. Since then English Heritage, which owns and maintains the monument, has forbidden access at the solstice.

Many visitors are understandably disappointed at not being able to wander around the stones. Meanwhile, the parking and other facilities for visitors have been much criticised: the Public Accounts Committee of the House of Commons has called them 'a national disgrace'. In the summer of 1994 English Heritage came up with a bold plan, which would involve demolishing all the existing facilities, building a new visitor centre two miles from the stones, and providing an electric tram to take visitors to an underground centre with an observation post. There would be open access to the stones once more, based on the belief that only the keenest visitors would be prepared to walk to the site, and that numbers would not be a problem.

Creating a boardwalk in Sefton Nature Reserve: many countryside areas now need protection from erosion.

It's a costly but imaginative solution to a dilemma that, on a much smaller scale, many other places are having to deal with, but with fewer resources and only limited scope for action. Kynance Cove on the Lizard Peninsula, owned by the National Trust, is a case in point.

A popular coastal beauty spot in a spectacular position, which has attracted visitors since the eighteenth century, its cliff areas abound in flora and fauna, with some heathland especially rich in species of plants. In the spring and summer months the cove is immensely popular – it now attracts as many as 110,000 visitors in that period. Their continuing presence has turned much of the clifftop into rock and bare soil. The National Trust embarked on a programme of re-routing visitors and restoring the damaged footpaths, but was hindered in its efforts by the presence of a commercially owned and unsightly café and shop on the site. Only after it was able to buy and demolish the buildings, and take over the linked car park and road, was it possible to fully control the movement and level of visitors. Today the erosion and damage to vegetation is minimal.

The Lake District is another area where physical damage has been extensive. In the national park there are 1,860 miles of footpaths, many of them heavily eroded by the millions of annual visitors. Now a new Lake District Tourism and Conservation Partnership has been set up, to try to protect the local landscape, in part by raising funds to enable much-needed conservation work to take place in the eroded areas.

Wildlife and habitats

Such damage can have an effect on habitats and plants, reducing diversity, even causing species to become extinct. Birds and animals can also be at risk. Many of the wilder areas of the country are attractive to visitors precisely because of the wildlife to be found there. Here again, usually unintentionally, their presence can have a negative impact; for instance, by causing a disturbance to the breeding patterns of birds, leading to a decline in their numbers, and even extinction.

This has been a particular problem in the Area of Outstanding Natural Beauty covering the Norfolk Coast. Here there are many breeds of birds of national and international significance, such as terns, redshanks, oystercatchers, and avocets, some of which nest and breed on the region's beaches and saltmarshes. The present balance between visitors and wildlife is felt to be precarious in some parts of the AONB, and the situation is likely to become worse as planned local road improvements bring more visitors to this still relatively unspoilt area. There is concern that the wildlife resources could be seriously damaged unless some action is taken very soon.

So one of the priorities of the recently established Norfolk Coast Project is to find ways of reversing this trend, by persuading visitors to consider going to the less popular areas of the AONB. Its solution has been to divide the land into three categories – fragile with heavy visitor pressure, fragile but with fewer pressures, and more robust with few pressures – and to try to channel visitors into the more robust areas .

Diverting visitors

But if open access is to remain as a right, controlling the flow of visitors is not a straightforward matter. For one thing, people have to be convinced that the less popular areas are as worth visiting as the honeypots. This is the kind of issue that has been exercising those involved in the Wiltshire Tourism Project. The county has 75 tourist attractions, some of which – Stonehenge Down, Salisbury Cathedral, Stourhead, Avebury, Longleat – have international status and are heavily visited. But there are other places of potentially great attraction that are less popular, including some in the Cranborne Chase and the West Wiltshire Downs AONB. Three areas seen as having potential for an increase in tourism without damaging the landscape are the Cotswold fringe, the Kennet and Avon Canal, and the North Wessex Downs.

One part of the Wiltshire strategy is to promote these areas more vigorously; another is to ensure a greater variety of accommodation to suit the needs of cyclists and ramblers who might be attracted to them. Within the North Wessex Downs AONB, a number of initiatives have been started under the auspices of the Wiltshire Downs Project, to lure visitors to lesser-known spots. These include the encouragement of off-road horse riding on the ancient byways, providing improved information about specialist interest weekend and holiday breaks, and establishing a varied arts programme in the area.

In some of these places, strategies for controlling the volume and movement of visitors are beginning to have an effect. But there are still plenty where numbers are steadily increasing, to an extent that is jeopardising any enjoyment people may gain from a visit.

Blueprint for Change: Greece

Since 1991, the organisation Friends of the Ionian has been working to make tourism in the Ionian Islands more sustainable, by bringing together local communities, tour operators and tourists. It encourages visitors to explore alternative locations in order to lessen pressure on popular resorts and fragile coasts.

Its projects include:

* Maps and trails produced with local communities, giving information on villages, customs and landscapes.
* Regular beach clean-ups with tour companies, local councils and schools.
* Cultural activities involving visits to vineyards, olive presses and coffee shops.
* Producing pamphlets on Ionian flowers, butterflies, birds and other wildlife.
* Publishing wildlife guides sponsored by tour operators, outlining easy walks close to popular resorts.

Inappropriate development

Development in England has occurred at a startling rate at different times. According to the Council for the Protection of Rural England, between 1945 and 1990 the urban part of the country grew by an area greater than the size of Berkshire, Hertfordshire, Oxfordshire and Greater London put together. Despite the greater awareness of the harm that tourist developments can cause, they will consume thousands of acres of undeveloped land by the end of the century. Efforts are being made to contain the situation in the most vulnerable coastal and countryside regions. In Wales and other countries, for instance, exclusion zones have been put round the coast, preventing planning applications and developments. In England the National Trust has also helped to keep the developers at bay: in Wharfedale in North Yorkshire, for example, it recently bought the last working farm, which would otherwise have been broken up and made into yet more holiday homes in an area already full of them.

There has also been strong resistance to planning applications for tourist developments in national parks. One of the most controversial of these was for a golf course at Catholes in the Yorkshire Dales National Park, which was strongly resisted by the Ramblers' Association and other conservation groups. There have also been examples of national parks refusing to sanction the building of what they see as inappropriate equestrian centres and other buildings.

In recent years the policy of the parks and other bodies has been to encourage the use of existing buildings to cater for tourists, especially when they are used for accommodation. The Youth Hostels Association, for example, has with minimal alterations converted a variety of buildings into hostels – castles, cottages, chapels and mills. In many cases this has prevented their demolition, or a drastic and inappropriate change in their appearance. Meanwhile camping barns, using existing farm buildings, have become increasingly popular in the national parks since they were launched in the 1980s. The larger bunkhouse barns pioneered more recently in the Yorkshire Dales, and now being developed on Dartmoor, also provide good examples of an appropriate use of buildings that already fit in to the landscape.

Sustainable tourism in the national parks is likely to be developed further as a result of a new initiative by the Countryside Commission. In the summer of 1994 it appointed consultants to look at the plans, policies and programmes of the Yorkshire Dales National Park in relation to sustainable tourism goals. The exercise is being treated as a trial run: the recommendations that emerge will be examined for the lessons that can be learned by the other national parks.[5]

Beside the sea

The traditional coastal resorts in the UK are not what they were. Their decline in popularity has a number of causes. One of these is undoubtedly the state of the sea water, heavily contaminated in many places by raw sewage and other pollutants. In 1993, for instance, 24 out of 80 beaches at 40 resorts failed to meet the European Union's minimum health standards. The resorts included many of the top UK attractions: Blackpool, Skegness, Weston-super-Mare, Colwyn Bay, Brighton and others.

But these and other resorts have also been hit hard by the dramatic increase in the number of people taking holidays abroad, and the demand for different kinds of domestic holidays. Immediately after the Second World War, 75% of holidays were on the coast; the figure is now 16%.[6] Projections for visitor numbers show a decline except in the case of two categories of resort: the large mass-market resorts catering for the traditional 'bucket-and-spade' holiday-maker, and small 'heritage' resorts attracting the AB1 market.

Many people in the tourist industry, not all of them with a vested interest in seeing a revival in the popularity of the resorts, argue that the best sustainable practice of all is to encourage tourists to return to them. Millions of people stay in a relatively small number of resorts every year: were they suddenly to go elsewhere in significant numbers, the argument runs, the impact on other places would be devastating. As the director of the British Resorts Association Peter Hampson puts it: 'The majority of these resorts were designed, built and further developed as tourist locations. Whatever the market, it has to be better to channel tourism into purpose-built resorts than try to manage it in more fragile environments. If the resorts flourish, it will leave other areas free to be enjoyed by smaller groups of tourists.'[7]

Some of the resorts are now making sustained efforts to woo the tourists back. The Lincolnshire Coast Partnership has recently been set up precisely for this purpose. Tourism is the lifeblood of this part of Lincolnshire, employing 21,000 people. One aim is to extend the tourist season beyond its present twenty-week period by encouraging off-peak holidays, to try to even out demand, and avoid business having to be turned away during the peak periods. Skegness, the area's principal resort, was one of the first planned in the country, and is currently the fifth largest, with 100,000 bed spaces. The partnership, launched in the summer of 1993, is working to revitalise the town's foreshore, and help local businesses improve the quality of their services.

Many of the resorts, especially the Victorian and Edwardian ones, have been decaying for many years, and have gone distinctly down-market. Several are now trying to address what they call their 'image problem'. This may, paradoxically, mean drawing attention to areas outside the resort itself in order to broaden its appeal. Weston-super-Mare in Avon, once the traditional holiday resort for the lower-middle and working classes of the industrial Midlands and south Wales, provides an example of this strategy. A Tourist Development Action Programme was recently set up to find ways of improving the resort's environment and its 'heritage potential'. In seeking funding for its work, the TDAP team suggested that 'it may be appropriate to attempt to pursue the emerging "green" and health-conscious markets, and to aim to link the resort more closely with its wider rural hinterland – the Mendips, Somerset levels and mystic "Avalon".'[8]

Code for Tourists: The Himalayas

The UK body Tourism Concern has cooperated with Nepal's Anapurna Conservation Area Project to produce a set of guidelines for tourists, aimed at preserving the unique environment and ancient cultures of the Himalayas. The code expresses the wishes and needs of the people living in the area. Its suggestions include:

- Limit deforestation – make no open fires.
- Remove litter, burn or bury paper.
- Keep local water clean and avoid using pollutants.
- Leave plants to flourish in their natural environment.
- Help guides and porters to follow conservation measures.
- When taking photographs, respect privacy and ask permission.
- Respect holy places – preserve what you have come to see.
- Follow local customs for eating, greeting, giving and receiving.
- Observe standard food and bed charges.
- Don't encourage begging: instead give a donation to a project, health centre or school.

In similar fashion, the Sussex resort of Eastbourne is making efforts to shed its geriatric image and reverse the drop in its tourist trade. A campaign by businesses and tourist operators designed to shock the town into action, under the headline 'Eastbourne – the Last Resort?', showed mock pictures of a collapsed pier, 'closing down' signs in front of stores, and run-down terraces packed with 'for sale' notices. As a result an Eastbourne Marketing Group was set up, with the aim of winning back 70,000 visitors a year, and creating a younger, more dynamic image for the town.

Starting from scratch

The people involved in these and other tourism initiatives described in this book are all too often engaged in a damage limitation exercise. A chance to begin at the beginning and learn from the mistakes of others is not given to many. But this is precisely the opportunity that has arisen for those involved in the creation of the National Forest, and of the twelve community forests which are beginning to be created around the UK.

The National Forest is a hugely ambitious scheme now taking shape on the sites of two ancient forests lying between Birmingham, Derby and Leicester. The aim is to create the forest out of two hundred square miles of countryside, much of it at present marred by sand and gravel workings and the aftermath of the coalmines. Based on the New Forest in Hampshire, the result will be a mosaic of farms, woods, towns and villages. The landscape is not just being conserved and improved, but re-shaped for a number of purposes – among them tourism in all its forms. Many eyes will be upon the project, to see how it grapples with the challenge of providing access for everyone, while ensuring that no serious damage is inflicted on the forest, or on the lives of the people who live in it.

Towards the Millennium

Wales

While Wales is mainly a rural country, it's one that offers visitors a great variety of coast and countryside within a comparatively small area, much of it of a unique wildness and beauty. As in England, tourism has caused many problems. In addition, alongside anxieties about how tourism is affecting the physical environment and the economic life and well-being of rural communities in the principality, there is also concern about its impact on Welsh culture and language.

The quality of the Welsh rural and coastal landscape is evident in the statistics on designated areas. The three national parks in the Brecon Beacons, the Pembrokeshire Coast and Snowdonia, together with the five Areas of Outstanding Natural Beauty – the Gower Peninsula, the Clwydian Range, the Anglesey Coast, the Lleyn Peninsula and the Wye Valley – together cover a quarter of the land, a higher proportion than anywhere else in the UK. Some 40% of the coastline is protected and conserved under the 'heritage coast' designation, and there are also 45 National Nature Reserves, 730 Sites of Special Scientific Interest, and 2,700 scheduled ancient monuments.

Tourism is a major industry in Wales, with 95,000 jobs providing employment for around 9% of the workforce within a population of 2.9 million. In 1993 the country attracted around 7.7 million visitors from the UK, of whom 70% came for a holiday. In 1992 some 640,000 visitors came from overseas. The coastal regions are especially popular: nearly 51% of domestic holiday-makers stayed overnight by the sea in 1993.

As elsewhere, the negative impacts of tourism are visible in a limited number of places and at certain times of the year, and are similar in kind

Snowdon from Crib Goch.

if not always in scale to those in other parts of the UK: pressure of visitor numbers on the landscape, traffic congestion, litter and pollution, intrusive leisure developments, and damage to marine life. Steps are now being taken, in the national parks and elsewhere, to try to alleviate these problems, and limit or reverse some of the damage.

Some of the most serious problems are to be found in Snowdonia, which has 13 million day visits a year. Footpath erosion has reached crisis point: in some places visitors have worn a path 25 feet wide. Wildlife habitats have been destroyed and rare plants trampled underfoot. The human damage has been especially noticeable on Snowdon itself, where at least half a million people a year climb up the six paths to the summit. There now has to be an almost continuous programme of footpath repair and maintenance, with two gangs of estate workers out on the paths for most of the year putting huge slabs of volcanic rock into place. Meanwhile the National Trust, a major landowner within the national park, has launched an appeal to prevent Snowdonia 'turning into a commercial wasteland or a lifeless museum'. It plans to spend £11 million by the end of the century on a programme of restoration which will include stone walling, hedge laying and planting, footpath repair, the protection of wildlife habitats, and the acquisition of land of particular beauty which is under threat.

The national park authority has recently prepared a Sustainable Tourism Action Plan for Snowdonia. In the Brecon Beacons, where the number of visitors is also creating problems, the authority's new five-year plan involves a 'Green Tourism' strategy, the implementation of which is now being discussed. Meanwhile the Mid Wales Tourism Action Group is busy formulating a sustainable tourism development strategy for mid Wales. A draft version says that sustainable principles are 'a basic theme permeating the entire strategy', and calls for the tourism industry 'to take a more proactive role in the protection and management of the wider countryside, and to involve the local communities to a greater degree in such activity'.

This growing interest in sustainable tourism is also reflected in the strategy document *Tourism 2000*, which after lengthy and widespread consultation was published by the Wales Tourist Board (WTB) in the spring of 1994. Although there was considerable disappointment within some environmental bodies about the final version – critics felt it was less radical and imaginative than it might have been – the WTB has at least put the question of environmental protection at the heart of its strategy for the first time, and acknowledged the need to work to sustainable principles. 'We must ensure that new tourism developments and initiatives are sustainable and respect the need of the environment,' it states. It also recognises that in rural areas there is a danger of an oversupply of tourism facilities, and that existing and new tourism businesses should be better integrated into the local economy.

The ultimate test of course will be to see what kind of tourism development the Wales Tourist Board actually encourages, or supports financially. In the strategy it identifies several headings under which new development action programmes could be considered for grant-aid, including coastal resort regeneration, historic towns, country holidays and urban tourism. It also aims to identify areas of special need where tourism development might help the process of economic regeneration, such as in the old mining areas in the South Wales Valleys, and in West Wales and South Gwynedd.

There are over 350 beaches in Wales, the majority small and isolated. As elsewhere in the UK, there have been problems for many of the larger designated beaches to meet the public health standards set by the European Community's Bathing Water Directive. Visitors are becoming more conscious of such measures, and are influenced by the publicity given annually to the UK's 'best' and 'worst' beaches. Here Wales is ahead of other countries: its programme of improvements, due for completion by the end of the century, will, according to *Tourism 2000*, give the principality the cleanest beaches in Europe.

One initiative the board is already involved in, with a number of partner organisations, is the development of a sustainable tourism strategy for mid Wales. Another is a demonstration project looking at ways of linking a range of rural tourist accommodation with environmentally sensitive use of the countryside, where visitors use public transport, walk, cycle or horse-ride. Two regions have been picked out for pilot treatment: rural Dwyfor and the Welsh Marches, which includes a section of the Offa's Dyke National Path.

Tourism 2000 pinpoints the importance of involving local communities in the development of tourism appropriate to their area. A striking example of this philosophy in action is the well-established Mid Wales Festival of the Countryside (see page 89). On a smaller scale, this has also been the basis of a rural tourism initiative in North Wales, where local people in the Hiraethog area have been heavily involved in promoting cultural tourism, with a restored estate village at its centre, and 'Welsh

Evenings' among the attractions.

Another project with community involvement at its heart is the more recent rural tourism strategy developed under the banner of SPARC, the South Pembrokeshire Partnership for Action with Rural Communities. This initiative covers forty rural towns and villages in an area of south-west Wales which has been badly affected by the recession in farming, and which, despite its natural beauty and its rich heritage, has in the past received few visitors.

The SPARC strategy is to develop appropriate kinds of small-scale tourism in a sustainable manner, while helping to regenerate the area economically. Its 'holistic' approach – acknowledging the inter-connectedness of tourism, the environment, the local economy, and community aspirations – is built on the direct involvement of around a thousand local people, who decide on their needs and the opportunities they wish to explore. The consultative process is considered crucial: each village has set up a community association which, by means of a community appraisal, identifies its strengths and weaknesses, and produces an action plan for attracting visitors. The result has been an impressive range of completed projects for what has become known as the Landsker Borderlands. These range from 150 miles of waymarked footpaths and bridleways to the restoration of old buildings, from the creation of a visitor centre to the establishment of a walking festival, from the setting up of an activity and specialist holiday bureau to the creation of five themed routes for walkers across the countryside.

While the Landsker Borderlands as yet have no problems with visitor pressure, such problem do arise in certain parts of the Wye Valley in Gwent, an Area of Outstanding Natural Beauty with an international reputation. Honeypot areas such as Symonds Yat Rock, with its 400,000 visitors a year, and Tintern Abbey are overcrowded, especially on summer weekends; walkers, horse-riders and mountain bikers are causing erosion to paths; there are conflicts between different user groups on the Wye itself. Meanwhile visitor numbers and outdoor activities are predicted to increase.

These are just some of the factors that have prompted the creation of the most recent sustainable tourism initiative in Wales. The Wye Valley

Tourism and Conservation project, established early in 1994, is an attempt to build up greater understanding between conservation bodies and tourism businesses, and to minimise conflicts between different user-groups. So far two public seminars have been held, at which different groups have aired their views on issues of potential conflict or concern. Rather than aiming to increase the number of visitors, the emphasis is on trying to get people to stay longer in the area by improving the quality of information, interpretation, accommodation and public transport, and to encourage visitors to support conservation more actively. The outcome of the project is likely to prove a good test of the principles of sustainable tourism, since most of the problems that can be thrown up by tourism can be found in the area.

One issue that does not arise in the Wye Valley, perhaps because of its proximity to the English border, is that of the Welsh language. Although there are anxieties in other parts of Wales that tourism could pose a threat to the language, other influences – such as modernisation, the spread of popular culture, migration, and the spread of second homes – are seen as more potentially damaging. However, Welsh speakers play a comparatively small part in tourism. So efforts are being made to increase the use of Welsh in tourism and to get Welsh speakers more involved. Menter a Busnes (Initiative and Business) is an organisation which campaigns to change Welsh speakers' perceptions of business, and persuade more of them to move into tourism. Local groups and societies are looking at ways of making more positive use of the language. This makes considerable sense, since it appears that many visitors, especially from overseas, are attracted to Wales not just because of the outstanding landscape, but because of its separate language, and its strong traditions in music and the arts.

The Mid Wales Festival of the Countryside

This festival, now nine years old, has become a well-known and well-supported part of the Welsh tourism landscape. Although it offers people plenty to be festive about, 'festival' seems a slightly misleading term for a programme of some six hundred events taking place in the heart of

Wales which already extends over seven months, and now threatens to stretch across most of the year.

It was launched in 1985 as a contribution to the World Conservation Strategy under the direction of the Welsh conservation foundation Cynefin. The word, which is one that lies behind much of Welsh culture, translates very roughly as a mixture of a sense of place, or a feeling of being at home, of 'rightness'. It is also emblematic of the spirit of the festival, which is a coordinated attempt at putting sustainable tourism principles into action over an area covering 40% of the land in Wales.

The programme is an extremely varied one, which broadly breaks down into six kinds of rural activities, events and attractions:

- Nature and wildlife – including nature reserve visits, bird and mammal watching, and natural history courses.
- Walks and guides – a range of guided and self-guided walks.
- Rural rides – these include narrow-gauge railway trips, white-water rafting, pony trekking and mountain biking.
- History and industry – covering visits to working farms, forests, reservoirs, markets and water mills, castles and other historic sites.
- Arts and crafts – includes art, sculpture and photographic exhibitions and visits to craft workshops.
- Eating out – at selected cafés and restaurants which can offer regional cuisine.

The festival is essentially a participatory one: its programme is planned and delivered by a very wide range of local organisations, groups and individuals. The role of the central festival team is to coordinate and market the programme, identify opportunities for innovation and new events, and to provide a year-round support and advisory service. It also compiles and publishes annually the free magazine which acts as the main promotional vehicle for the festival.

The festival's basic aim is to 'encourage the development of environ-mental common sense and recreational opportunities, as well as economic prosperity', by advocating 'informed access to the countryside and responsible development of new products and events'. The message seems to be having an impact: whereas in its first year the festival attracted 90,000, by 1993 the figure had risen to close on 300,000. It has also created the equivalent of 20 full-time jobs, and generates a £5 million annual turnover for the rural economy of the region.

Arwel Jones, director of the festival, says that feedback from a questionnaire inserted in the 1994 programme has been very positive. 'The information centres have been approving, as have the events operators,' he says. 'As for the public, the general reaction has been, "Don't change it, we love it."'

The organisers are now looking to strengthen the autumn programme, and are even considering introducing a winter element. Their plans include working out new 'green tourism packages' with farmhouse groups, based on quiet recreation; and producing a handbook which will pass on to others their experience of developing events and encouraging community involvement.

A review of the festival is to be completed shortly. It comes at a time of changing political structures, when tourist and development agencies and local authorities are having to look at their new responsibilities or reconsider their budgets. The festival team is having to talk to all of its partners about their future relationships. But it's hard to imagine that such a successful venture, which shows that sustainable tourism can be a reality in such a setting, won't carry on changing and developing well beyond the timescale of *Tourism 2000*.

6 Getting There

'The tourism culture is increasingly car-bound'

Patrick Wright [1]

One of the main obstacles to developing sustainable tourism, at least in the developed countries, is the widespread use of the car by visitors and holiday-makers.

Alongside the lorry and the aeroplane, the car is the most polluting and least energy-efficient of all forms of transport. Road traffic is the fastest growing source of gases such as carbon dioxide, nitrogen oxide, and others which contribute to global warming. Pollution from traffic contributes significantly to acid rain, which damages trees, plants and buildings. Increasingly it's also having a damaging effect on people's health, especially that of children, elderly people, and those with asthma and other respiratory problems. When it comes to the impact on the environment and use of resources, the car scores very badly indeed.

In a small island like Britain the problem is already an acute one, and is likely to become worse if present trends continue. Recent surveys and forecasts show that:

- Over 20 million cars are now registered, and the number could almost double by the year 2025.
- Car mileage has risen by 45% in the last decade.
- In 1990, 80% of trips to the countryside were made by car.
- Car traffic causes 19% of the country's carbon dioxide emissions, and 45% of nitrogen oxide emissions.
- World Health Organisation limits are regularly exceeded in many UK cities.

Yet the car is also a means of gaining access to places that may otherwise be beyond our reach, or involve too long or complicated a journey. It's not surprising then that we're loath to stop using the car for such journeys, despite the frustrations of increasing congestion on the roads. So, as car ownership relentlessly increases, the pressure becomes more intense to find ways of encouraging people to use other forms of transport when they adopt the mantle of the tourist.

The Countrygoer Project shows one way of doing it. It's a campaign set up to help people become more aware of the opportunities that exist to take the train or bus into the countryside. It publishes a magazine that highlights good transport schemes around the country, together with a guide with up-to-date travel information for every county. Colin Speakman, from Transport for Leisure, which coordinates the project, believes that using public transport can often make for a better travelling experience. 'There is less stress, more space, better views from elevated windows allowing the passenger to see above walls and hedges, and flexibility, especially for the rambler who doesn't have to return to a parked (and possibly burgled) car. You also have an opportunity to meet your fellow travellers, including local people.'

A rail alternative

Among the alternatives, the train is one of the most attractive options. Unfortunately, the railway network in Britain has been gradually cut back over the last thirty years. Services to the more remote rural areas have been particularly affected. With privatisation now introduced, the pressure to increase profits may result in the closure of even more lines. Yet the picture is not entirely gloomy. Railway enthusiasts have succeeded in keeping open or re-opening many lines. In doing so they have in some places created not just a tourist attraction, but an alternative means of transport for both visitors and local people.

One of the most successful stories is that of the 72-mile Settle-Carlisle railway line, which provides spectacular views of upland landscape, as well as a vital link from nearby cities to the rural communities in the Yorkshire Dales National Park. In the 1980s the line was threatened with closure, but was saved after nationwide protests. The number of users increased during and after the successful campaign: the line now carries half a million 'passenger trips' a year, 80% of which are for tourism and leisure uses. The new company set up to run the line believes it can double this number if facilities and information are improved, and if links are made between the railway and the small communities and market towns that it passes through. Since the trains are often full at summer weekends, it's aiming to promote off-season and weekday travel, in order to spread the load. It sees the use of the railway and links with local transport as 'the key to potential car-free tourism' within a sustainable approach.

Steam enthusiasts have kept many branch lines open, creating a useful transport alternative for tourists.

Enthusiasts have been notably successful in keeping branch lines open so that steam trains can continue to operate. Almost all regions in the UK now have at least one preserved line running through the countryside in the summer. Among the best known are the Bluebell Line in Sussex, the Ffestiniog Railway in Snowdonia, and the twenty-mile long West Somerset Railway that meanders between the Quantock and the Bredon Hills. There are plans for many of these to be extended and, most importantly for access, to be linked to the main rail network. Others, such as the line running to Bolton Abbey in the Yorkshire Dales, are linking up with specific tourist attractions.

Some of the new regional railway companies are beginning to collaborate with tourism initiatives. An interesting recent example is the partnership set up to promote the Tarka Line in rural Devon. (See case study, page 49.) Many other lines are now helping to improve access to and lessen car use in the countryside.

The Heart of Wales Line, which runs between Shrewsbury and Swansea, is a good example. The train stops on request at many rural halts; there are good links with coach services to the Elan Valley from Llandridod Wells; and bicycles can be taken on board or hired along the way. In West Yorkshire, two railway and walking schemes enable you to stop off and walk from station to station in the countryside. One of the more unusual journeys is that provided by the Hebridean Heritage Service, where you can sit in a special observation car to observe the lochs and mountains between Inverness and the Kyle of Lochalsh. And one much-visited attraction on the Scotland/England border, the celebrated Blacksmith's Shop at Gretna, is now accessible again by rail: the station there, closed for twenty years, re-opened in the summer of 1994.

One of the larger rail tourism projects with sustainable tourism objectives is the Devon and Cornwall Rail Partnership. The project aims to encourage greater use of the two counties' rural railways, including the Tamar Valley Line and the Looe Valley Line. It's evidently played a part in reducing rural road traffic, not only increasing passenger use but spreading it more evenly outside the July/August peaks. Significantly, early passenger surveys showed that 53% of respondents could have made their journey by car. It was also clear from the same research that the lines were helping to provide access to the countryside for non-car users. Crucial to progress has been the coordination of links from the railway to the countryside, including bus links, trails and footpaths, cycleways, river ferry services, and private railways.

In the fast-developing National Forest, where encouraging people to use public transport is a fundamental principle, there will also be a strong emphasis on travelling by train. A new rail route is planned for the area, together with six new stations containing plenty of car-parking space.

Boarding the bus

In many parts of the UK the bus is the only alternative to the car. Here bus companies and tourism bodies are getting together, to their mutual benefit. There's the imaginative initiative by the North York Moors National Park, where visitors' cars were becoming a nuisance to local residents at weekends. The scheme enables buses to pick visitors up on a Sunday from some of the larger towns around the park, and shuttle them from a single meeting-point across the moors. The park authority has usefully provided guided walks directly linked to the services, and there are hopes that the arrangement can be extended to weekdays. In similar fashion, backed by the slogan 'Leave Your Car Behind!', the principal bus operator in the Lake District has produced a free leaflet, describing eight easy walks that link in with bus services in the heart of the Lakes. The Friends of the Lake District has also produced a booklet outlining public transport services.

Providing good, up-to-date information is clearly an important element in any campaign to woo people away from their cars. The 'discovery trail' leaflets produced through the Lizard Peninsula Project in Cornwall offer a good model. The Lizard, Britain's most southerly peninsula, with its miles of woodland, high cliffs and coastal footpaths, is a notorious honeypot in the summer months. The attractive, high-quality leaflets – they include coverage of the Naturalist's Trail, the Wrecker's Trail and the Fisherman's Trail – link the history of the place to the local bus service, making it easier to plan an interesting day out travelling by bus and walking, while leaving your car outside the area.

Visitor pressure has also been the spur for the Surrey Hills Visitor Project, one of the pilot projects set up in response to *Maintaining the Balance*. The popularity of such places as Leith Hill – the highest point in southern England – and Box Hill, situated in this designated Area of Outstanding Natural Beauty, is causing traffic congestion and creating parking problems, especially at weekends. So a key element in the project has been to make public transport to and within the area more attractive. Vintage buses from the 1950s have been providing extra Sunday and public holiday services, which enable people from London and around to visit stately homes, working farms, wine estates and local villages. A special Sunday ticket, allowing travel on buses throughout the county including the vintage ones, has helped to make the service popular with day trippers.

Many bus services in rural areas have deteriorated in recent years, forcing people living in the country to rely on a car. But many can't afford to run one, and have to use what services there are. So encouraging tourists to use the local buses helps to keep the services going for the benefit of local people. Some tourism projects, such as the North Pennines Tourism Partnership, are giving priority in their new maps and promotional literature to users of public transport, emphasising bus and train routes rather than information for car users.

Changing Transport: Austria

With 1.3 million visitors a year, the Grossglockner Hochalpenstrasse in the Hohe Tauern National Park is the second most visited site in Austria, providing a fine panoramic view of the Eastern Alps.

Most visitors travel to it by car during the summer months. In order to reduce pollution levels and the increasing traffic problems caused by breakdowns, the publicly owned company that owns and manages the pass aimed to cut down the use of cars, and increase that of public transport. Bus services were reinstated, additional routes arranged, and a special family rate introduced. Meanwhile the cost for cars was increased.

Use of public transport rose from 30% to 40%; the target by the year 2000 is 70%. The eventual aim is to close the road to cars, and to allow only shuttle buses, coaches and public buses to use it. Meanwhile many parking areas are being landscaped and reduced in size.

On two wheels

Aside from walking, cycling is easily the most environmentally friendly form of transport. Apart from being one of the most healthy forms of activity, it also helps to reduce levels of pollution. Despite the UK government's failure to consider cyclists' needs in the way that governments of other countries have done, cycling is increasingly becoming an option for tourists. Cycle routes are being opened up, hiring facilities are becoming more widespread, and cycle owners are now able to put their machines on many trains and buses.

One of the earliest and most ambitious schemes to help cyclists is the traffic-free network created by Sustrans. For ten years the organisation – it stands for Sustainable Transport – has been building what it calls 'paths for people'. These are routes designed exclusively for cyclists, walkers and disabled people, making use of disused railway lines, canal towpaths, forest tracks and riversides. The 300 miles already completed provide a link between towns and cities and the open countryside. The idea is proving popular: Sustrans' first creation, the Bristol and Bath Railway Path, now carries over one million journeys a year. Another, the Consett and Sunderland Railway Path, is not just a traffic-free alternative: along its seventeen miles can be found pieces of eye-catching sculpture by artists such as Andy Goldsworthy.

Cycling's increased popularity owes much to the phenomenal rise of the mountain bike. But its use, as we have seen, has often led to conflicts with walkers, or with local people. Some initiatives are designed to reduce the likelihood of such conflicts. In the Isle of Wight, for instance, the council has produced especially for mountain bikers a series of illustrated maps of byways and bridleways, with 15 recommended circular routes, and interpretative information covering two hundred miles of traffic-free routes on the island. The idea is to prevent conflict with walkers by ensuring the footpaths remain clear for them.

The most recent initiative designed to prevent such conflict is in the Lake District National Park. A pilot scheme launched in the summer of 1994 has wardens patrolling on mountain bikes, handing out advice and cycling codes of conduct to mountain bikers. In Snowdonia, where there have been many conflicts between cyclists and walkers, a voluntary agreement involving diverting mountain bike users to alternative routes to avoid the paths leading directly to the summit has significantly reduced the amount of conflict with walkers. At Kielder Water on the edge of the Northumberland National Park, a small cycle-hire company that has created specially graded trails on Forestry Commission land makes a point of giving tuition in responsible mountain biking to hirers.

The Staffordshire Moorlands Council has also produced information about routes aimed especially at novice cyclists.

Bike owners are often prevented from using their machines in the countryside because of the problem of transporting them. The railway companies are still reluctant to provide more than very limited space for bicycles, even when the demand is obvious. Cost is obviously a factor, as it was with the first bike-carrying bus service, which took machines from Manchester and Liverpool into the Yorkshire Dales and the Peak District, but which ended in 1992. A more successful venture has been in Northumbria, where dual-purpose buses travelling from Newcastle to Berwick can, for a nominal sum, take bicycles in the boot, giving people access to good cycling country along the unspoiled Northumbrian coastline.

For non-owners, hiring a bike for the day is an attractive option, and one for which opportunities are increasing all over the country. One of the best established of the services is in the Peak District National Park, which has four hire centres, and attracts 55,000 customers a year, both day visitors and longer-stay tourists. The centres, which make it possible to explore the Upper Derwent Valley and the Tissington Trail, have recently started providing trailers, which enable parents to take younger children out safely on their journeys.

Even the government is beginning at last to turn its attention to the idea of cycle routes. In 1994, after three years of discussion, it announced its intention to approve the country's first purpose-designed national trail for cyclists and horse-riders, along two hundred miles of the Pennine Bridleway.

The conservation bodies

Meanwhile, the main bodies that administer or own much-visited sites are taking steps to encourage visitors to use public transport where possible. English Heritage lists the relevant rail and bus services in its annual guide to its properties. The National Trust goes further, and offers discounts to visitors arriving by public transport. For instance, if you travel to Lydford Gorge or Castle Drogo in Devon, you are admitted at the party rate; there's a reduction in the price of entry at Ham House in

Richmond if you come by Riverbus; and there's a similar arrangement for rail travellers at the Cheshire house Dunham Massey. In addition, the trust runs its own steam train in West Yorkshire, which gives access to East Riddlesden Hall near Keighley; and a cycle-hire scheme in Norfolk that enables you to cycle between attractions. Some of the trust's properties also provide cycle racks or safe areas for the storage of bikes.

Walk and Ride: Germany

Through the Wandern ohne Gepäck and Radwandern ohne Gepäck schemes, most of Germany's well-established nature parks now offer visitors the opportunity to walk or cycle there unburdened by luggage, which is taken on by a single car to their next port of call.

Programmes for walkers and cyclists are devised by local tourist organisations, who undertake marketing and central booking, or by groups of places offering accommodation. Such packages, for which there is a great demand, allow visitors to travel individually on identified routes, following maps and waymarking, and armed with a booklet which acts as an interpretative guide to the park.

Visitors generally spend successive nights in accommodation no more than twelve miles apart, making the transportation of their luggage relatively easy. They usually select accommodation in advance from a range of hotels or bed and breakfast venues.

Managing the cars

Despite all these initiatives designed to encourage alternatives, and the growing awareness of the damage the car is doing to the environment, the fact has to be faced that most of us will still be using our car for such journeys in the immediate future. This is why the matter of 'transport management' now figures so prominently in the plans of those tourist agencies, tourism projects and conservation bodies that are exploring the possibilities of sustainable tourism.

Various strategies have been tried to deal with the problem. On Dartmoor the park authority has had some success in controlling the level and flows of traffic. They've introduced a 'route network' for the national park, which defines which roads are suitable for which kinds of traffic. One of these, designed specifically for coach and minibus drivers, has had significant success in reducing congestion. So too have other moves, such as downgrading certain roads. More recently, the Dartmoor Area Tourism Initiative has been encouraging coach drivers to visit the larger area rather than just the moor itself. It provides them with a handbook that includes suggested day and half-day tours, with accompanying interpretation.

Sometimes the solutions are more drastic. In Dovedale in the Peak District National Park, for example, cars have been actually banned at the busiest times of the year, and discussions are in hand about a year-round ban on one stretch of road. In the Lake District, a number of restrictions on car use are being actively considered, including restricting access to a road near Ambleside much used by pedestrians. A few of the least accessible villages in the West Country have been closed to traffic during the summer. At Kynance Cove, visited by 200,000 people a year, once full capacity has been reached the National Trust sometimes closes the site to further visitors.

Manipulating the use of car parks has been another way of controlling the numbers that visit a place, and so lessening the damage. Flatford Mill in Suffolk is a popular attraction because of Constable's paintings of the surrounding area and an exhibition of many of them at Bridge House near the mill. The National Trust, feeling that full capacity had been reached, made the decision not to extend the existing car park. In Dovedale, parking has been reduced from 750 to 400 spaces, while smaller, landscaped car parks have been built within reasonable distance of the dale. One of the current aims on Dartmoor is to stop any further increase in parking on those fragile sites in the national park where erosion has been severe, and to redistribute parking facilities more evenly. In Borrowdale and elsewhere in the Lake District, the National Trust is making travel by car more expensive by introducing charges for use of its car parks.

Park and ride schemes, which have been in place in certain towns and cities like Bath and Oxford for a number of years, are now being introduced in some rural areas or for coastal attractions. Such a facility will, for example, soon be introduced on the Isle of Purbeck in Dorset, which will reduce the pressure on parking space caused by the thousands who visit Corfe Castle. (See case study, page 33.)

Information can be another key to influence the journeys taken by car and coach drivers. Many route signs are put up to direct drivers along certain roads where traffic is less heavy, while marketing literature also stresses the least congested routes for access to popular places. A more recent technique for limiting the numbers of cars coming to an area is that known as 'de-marketing'. This may simply be a matter of emphasis in a promotional leaflet, where perhaps a picture of the most popular attraction in an area is replaced by one showing a less well-known destination. This has happened with the Quantock Hills in Somerset, a fragile environment which the West Country Tourist Board has agreed not to promote for that reason. For Flatford Mill, the National Trust has decided that there will be no signs for the attraction on major roads.

Sometimes the practice goes as far as having information about a place deleted or withdrawn from guidebooks and maps. For example, the village of Lacock, owned by the National Trust and visited by half a million people a year, has been omitted from the members' handbook – although Lacock Abbey and the Fox Talbot Museum of Photography, both on the edge of the village, are included. Similarly the Lyke Wake Walk, the famous long-distance path in North Yorkshire, which has had to be closed on several occasions to let the ground recover from the wear caused by thousands of walkers, has been left off Ordnance Survey maps. And for Dartmoor, road maps of the area no longer show attractive through routes: the result has been a reduction in through-traffic on some roads.

While many of these measures are proving effective in the short term, it's clear that in some areas they are doing little more than holding the line, while environments and communities are still suffering the adverse effects of car use. It may not be long before more fundamental measures will have to be introduced, resulting in a total ban on visitors' cars in many places, at least at certain times of the year. This has already happened in other countries: in the Black Forest in Germany, for instance, there are areas where minor roads are closed to all except local traffic, cyclists and walkers.

In recent months it's been possible to discern a shift in government thinking, and a belated recognition that firm measures are needed to effect a switch away from the 'culture of the car'. The report by the Royal Commission on Environmental Protection, published in the autumn of 1994, may compel the government to adopt targets for reducing car use and encouraging a greater use of public transport and bicycles. Ultimately the big question, and one not just concerned with tourism, remains: at what point are we prepared to accept that our right to drive our car anywhere we please may have to be restricted in order to prevent further damage to the environment? If present trends continue, and the government fails to introduce policies that tackle this issue, it's a question that is likely to be put to the test sooner rather than later.

Making the Links

Scotland

L ike Wales, Scotland is rightly celebrated for the beauty and wildness of its countryside. In the Highlands especially – the least densely populated area within the European Community – the lochs, glens and moors provide some of the grandest scenery to be found in Europe. Despite its extremely variable weather, the country is a great attraction to tourists from all over the world.

Happily, the remoteness of some areas has limited the damage done by tourism to the environment and to local communities. And by no means all of Scotland's environmental problems are caused by visitors: some of the most intractable have come about because of changing farming practices, over-forestation, and industrial pollution.

Yet visitors have created huge problems, and had an adverse impact on certain popular places, most notably the Cairngorms, Ben Nevis, Loch Lomond and other honeypot areas. Here the picture at certain times of the year is similar to that in England and Wales: traffic congestion and its attendant pollution, wildlife disturbance, litter, noise, and tension between visitors and residents. Footpath erosion has been a major problem: one estimate of the national repair bill is £750,000. In addition, in its mountain regions, many of which are more fragile than those in the Alps, the country is experiencing many of the environmental problems more usually associated with the popular ski resorts in Europe.

In 1993, Scotland attracted over 9 million visits from the UK, and a further 1.5 million from overseas. Visitor pressure also comes from the 85 million day-trips made every year by resident Scots, who tend to go to much the same places as the foreign tourists. Yet visitor surveys have

Eilean Donan Castle in the Highlands.

shown that more than 90% of the main likes of visitors are directly related to the quality of the natural environment, and that 82% put scenery at the top of their list. Meanwhile, there has been an overall decline in tourism in the last five years. How far this may be connected with the quality of the experience tourists get is currently a matter of some debate in Scotland.

Despite this fall-off, there's evidence of increasing interest in the idea of sustainable tourism. However it's clear that, as in other countries, there are different understandings of the concept. Duncan Bryden, a tourism and environment officer with a national remit, believes that many people have not yet grasped what it's about. 'It's not yet understood very well, but it's the buzz word people are putting on everything,' he says. 'Everyone has their own ideas about what it is, but they go down their own blinkered path. The economic developer sees it in terms of job creation, the environmental folk see it as habitat and wildlife protection, while a community sees it in terms of the survival of their language and culture. But if sustainable tourism means anything, it's about linking all these things together.'

One established initiative that has tried to make these links is the LOCUS project in Aberfeldy, in highland Perthshire (see page 110). But the spur for many of the projects now being developed or set up was the report *Tourism and the Scottish Environment: A Sustainable Approach*, produced in 1992 by the Scottish Tourism Coordinating Group. Based on widespread consultation amongst public and voluntary bodies, it showed clearly that pressure on the environment was growing. The report highlighted five issues that needed particular attention: footpath damage; the impact of caravans; the controversy surrounding ski centres; the intrusion of such activities as water and motor sports; and other kinds of environmental disturbance, such as that affecting sensitive bird species and habitats.

Following publication of the report, a task force was set up to promote the principles of sustainable tourism, which had been adopted by the Scottish Office. This group, consisting of several government bodies and departments, then identified pilot projects in ten areas in Scotland, where different approaches to tourism development, conservation and repair would be tried out.

The initiative that seems to have made the most progress so far is the Trossachs Trail, covering the wild highland area east and north-east of Loch Lomond, a region which includes the 'Rob Roy Country' made famous by Sir Walter Scott. The area suffers from many problems, including traffic congestion at peak periods, insensitive developments, deteriorating landscape, and poor-quality accommodation and services.

The Trossachs project, now in its second year, comes under the banner of the Rural Stirling Partnership. During its first year, the project concentrated on uncontentious remedial work, which was widely agreed locally to be necessary. This included repairing mountain footpaths, improving car parks, replacing tourist information points, clearing litter, and upgrading visitor centres.

The next phase is likely to be more problematic. 'The challenge is to find ways of getting the commercial tour operators involved,' says Steve Roderick, project manager for the partnership. 'It's been a bleak year for tourism, and most businesses are just trying to survive, they're very aware of the bank manager breathing down their necks. There's a tendency to simply rely on the volume of the market, so trying to get them interested in green ideas is quite a struggle. It's the usual story: the few good guys are on the ball, it's the majority we have to persuade. Very few are overtly green at this stage – although they all know now what we're doing.'

In order to raise awareness of the issues, the project has recently organised a series of workshops entitled How To Go Green. They offered suggestions of how to buy materials in bulk, and how best to attract custom from Germany and France, where such ideas are more widely accepted. The project also arranges environmental audits for businesses at minimal cost; advises them on ways of providing alternatives such as cycling holidays; and tries to make them aware of how their counterparts in other places are moving in this kind of direction.

Tourism and the Scottish Environment highlighted the issue of environmental damage at ski resorts, caused by visitor pressure and inappropriate and intrusive building, both controversial issues for some years now. The debate has been particularly intense over developments in the Cairngorms, generally acknowledged to be one of the finest areas in Western Europe for scenery, wildlife and mountain pursuits, and which has been identified as a potential World Heritage Site.

It has already been adversely affected by the creation of skiing and other sporting facilities. In 1991 widespread protests against plans to extend skiing facilities in the Northern Corries in the Cairngorms resulted in their being dropped. However, in the summer of 1994 the issue surfaced again, when the Cairngorm Chairlift Company published its plans for a funicular railway, to be complemented by a new interpretative centre 'designed to increase public awareness, understanding, appreciation and enjoyment of the mountain environment'. The Save the Cairngorms Campaign, an alliance of 15 conservation and recreation groups, has been fighting since 1988 to protect the Cairngorms. It believes that voluntary measures have failed, and that ultimately the UK government is responsible for failing to control the enormous powers of private landowners in this internationally significant region.

The debate continues over the Cairngorms. But a new problem has recently arisen in many of the skiing areas: how to control the growing number of visitors who use the ski-lifts in the summer to get up to and walk around the fragile mountain areas. The trend began at Aonach Mor on Ben Nevis; now other centres are looking at ways of diversifying in order to extend the tourist season. One result has been proposals for a tourism management programme for the Cairn Gorm summit, aimed at reducing the impact of visitors on the natural environment.

Erosion of the hill and mountain landscape has also been the spur for action in another of Scotland's beauty spots, the Isle of Skye. Here the wear and tear caused by walkers and climbers has been made worse by the wet climate, which can cause a dry path which crosses peaty ground to be turned into a running stream within a few hours. The Skye and Lochalsh Footpath Initiative, set up in the spring of 1994, involves major repair work being carried out over a period of eighteen months to some of the most scarred parts of the Cuillins and other upland areas. However, it's recognised that even this work will only scratch the surface, and that ways will need to be found to finance repair work on a continuing basis.

The Skye project is one of the pilots prompted by the *Tourism and the Scottish Environment* report. Another is an initiative centering on the celebrated Standing Stones of Callanish, on the island of Lewis in the Western Isles. Acknowledged to be the finest example of a neolithic/bronze age monument in Scotland, it is also, like Stonehenge, seen by many as a sacred landscape of religious and mystical significance. Plans for a new interpretative centre were recently announced, aimed at attracting up to 50,000 visitors a year to the stones. While the scheme is supported financially by groups such as Scottish Natural Heritage and Historic Scotland, the new centre, which is now under construction, has aroused some opposition locally. The newly formed pressure group Stonewatch, for instance, believes the centre could destroy the wilderness nature and the unique atmosphere of the site. As part of its opposition it is fighting to have signs removed and coach parties discouraged. The project team claims the centre will not have any impact on the setting of or access to the stones.

Other pilot programmes include a new development strategy for Loch Ness, where the emphasis will be on persuading some of the many thousands of casual visitors to stay longer by means of 'a sensitive expansion of tourist-related activities'; the continuing efforts of a community group in the Cumnock and Doon Valley in Strathclyde to turn a former mining area hit by industrial decline into a tourist attraction; and a project based in Kilmartin Glen on Argyll's Atlantic seaboard, where there are growing problems caused by tourist pressure.

While most of the concerns about the effects of tourism are focused on inland areas, there are also problems in some coastal regions, especially in relation to marine life. The most recent example is to be found in the Moray Firth in Ross and Cromarty, where as many as a hundred bottle-nosed dolphins – the largest in the world – have been sighted. For three years one small operator, Dolphin Ecosse, has been taking visitors out in a boat to watch the dolphins – in 1993 they took out around 3,500 people. But by the summer of 1994 the number of operators had increased dramatically to fourteen – almost more than the number of fishermen working in the Firth. There are worries that the boats could injure or kill the dolphins, or that their noise and presence could disturb their breeding and feeding patterns.

In an attempt to prevent the situation becoming serious, Scottish Natural Heritage has launched a Dolphin Awareness project, through which a voluntary code of conduct has been developed for the operators. Plans are also well advanced for a new high-tech visitor centre on the shores of the Firth, which will enable visitors to hear the dolphins live as well as to learn more about their way of life.

The centre is one of several projects being developed under the auspices of the LIFE programme, a European initiative which encourages countries to adopt principles of sustainable development. The Highland Region has secured funding for a number of projects which 'provide examples of good practice in the development of sustainable tourism and land use' in the Highlands. Projects funded for the first year of an initiative that runs until 1996 include:

- Organising repair and interpretation for the caves at Inchnadamph in Sutherland, where visitors have caused a lot of erosion.
- Enhancing the Great Glen cycle route between Fort William and Inverness by providing information and interpretation, and linking the route to small villages in the area.
- Providing interpretative facilities in the woodlands of Glen Affric, to cater for the growing interest in the history and development of Scotland's native woodlands.
- Setting up an accreditation system for wildlife holiday operators, to guard against uncontrolled growth that could damage the fauna in the region.

The progress of these, and of the many recent projects stimulated by the publication of *Tourism and the Scottish Environment*, will be watched closely, to see whether the sustainable principles on which they claim to be based remain intact in the face of pressures to halt Scotland's decline in tourism. There are still many in Scotland who remain sceptical about this increasing tourism activity, and who point to the danger of Scotland becoming one great theme park. Whatever the outcome, the last few years of the century seem set to establish whether or not Scotland can get the right balance between preserving its unique landscape and heritage, and heeding the economic imperatives of developing tourism.

The LOCUS Project, Aberfeldy, Perthshire

'Conveying the idea of our holistic approach to tourism is not easy,' says Brendan Murphy, one of the originators of the LOCUS project. 'People find it hard at first to get a handle on it.'

The project, based in the middle of Perthshire's glens and lochs, is a community-led initiative that differs in one simple way from other attempts to link tourism with rural regeneration: it's concerned with quality rather than quantity, it's not trying to attract more people to the area. Instead, by bringing visitors out of their cars and into contact with local people, it aims to inform them about the local places and people, in a way that will encourage their interest sufficiently to persuade them to return another time.

What is being created, Brendan Murphy suggests, is a 'virtuous circle': 'A better experience and an improved welcome for the visitor leads to a good reputation for the area, which leads to an increase in the desired type of tourist, which leads to longer stays and return visits, which leads to an extended season, which leads to more benefits to the host community and maintenance of the local environment, which leads to increased quality of interpretation and trail components, which leads to a better experience and an improved welcome for the visitor.'

The focus of the project is a series of interpretative trails around highland Perthshire, created in order to interest the visitor in the life of the community as well as its buildings and landscape. The project provides visitors with 'route packs', containing leaflets which give details of the trails, all of them devised by local people. Since another aim is to help new small business ventures to develop, information about them is made part of the trail. There are now five trails around the area open for use.

LOCUS, a community-run company started by a group of concerned farmers, businessmen and professionals, was formally launched in 1991. For most of its life it's been run entirely by unpaid volunteers: various kinds of land users, teachers, people with small businesses, conservationists, retired people, and some involved in the arts and crafts. This kind of structure ensures that control remains in local hands. But it can also create problems, since the energy and commitment of individuals with busy lives tends to ebb and flow. At present, for instance, there are doubts whether the retail operation, which sells packs, environmental literature and other goods, on which the project depends for its revenue, can continue indefinitely without some paid professional help.

This bottom-up approach has also, according to Brendan Murphy, brought the project into some disfavour with the regional tourist board. 'They don't like us trespassing on their bailiwick,' he says. 'Their argument is that Daddy knows best, we're the professionals, and if you want to market the area, you have to do it through us. They say it's a waste of resources for us to duplicate their efforts. But LOCUS is about local control.' This means regular involvement in brainstorming sessions, discussions about marketing strategy, the design of trails, and the identifying of new skills within the community.

Those involved in LOCUS believe that, though the number of visitors to the area has in fact increased, their impact on the environment, the local economy and the community is a positive one. The project has certainly attracted the attention of many others involved in tourism, both within and outside Scotland. Many have come to Aberfeldy to see for themselves if sustainable principles are really being upheld in this beautiful corner of Scotland.

7 Business Matters

'It's screaming at you if you're in the business, you realise it has to stop, something has to be done to make tourism beneficial.'

Noel Josephides, tour operator [1]

There are now some signs that people are waking up to the seriousness of the damage that tourism has caused in many places. Recognition of this fact is gradually changing attitudes, and forcing new ideas into the tourism equation. In the mass tourism sphere, for instance, certain operators are now acknowledging some responsibility for the state of the destinations to which they send people. Meanwhile, within the UK some tourism businesses, though still only a small minority, are being persuaded that sustainability could be good for them economically as well as environmentally.

The tour operators

In 1991, while they were researching their book *Holidays That Don't Cost the Earth*, John Elkington and Julia Hailes sent out an environmental questionnaire to some two hundred UK tour operators of all sizes. The results were not encouraging: 'In most firms it was clear that environmental issues had not yet been seriously addressed,' they reported. 'Worse, the recession not only reduced the number of people booking holidays but also, as a result, put the brakes on a number of the early green initiatives. Interestingly, very few of the firms that responded – whom we assume are among the better performers – had an environmental policy statement worthy of the name.'[2]

A subsequent workshop they held on tourism and the environment revealed an awareness that this issue was likely soon to move up the agenda. Since then a few operators have made some gestures towards environmental responsibility. Cox and King's, for example, makes donations to wildlife organisations, and trains its staff to be aware of social, cultural and environmental issues worldwide. Sunvil Holidays contributes around 10% of its profits to bodies such as the Friends of the Ionian and the Laona Project in Cyprus, and a few other small operators do the same. Laskarina Holidays encourages landlords and agents to renovate dilapidated old properties rather than build cheap concrete modern ones. British Airways Holidays has linked up with the World Conservation Union, and asks tourists to contribute to conservation work designed to preserve endangered species in several countries, pledging to provide matching donations. And Thomson, which has recently appointed an environment manager, has produced a pack aimed at getting hoteliers and others to think more carefully about waste management.

Special Tourism Area: India

India's national tourism policy involves creating special tourism areas. One of these is centred on the famous fort of Bekal in North Kerala. This is now set to become a tourist attraction as coastal land is developed for hotels, a convention centre, gardens, parks and leisure facilities.

The new centre will displace nearly two thousand families, and will demolish schools, temples and mosques. It will also adversely affect thousands of workers in other occupations who depend on fishing for their livelihoods.

A newly formed local action committee has called for the cancellation of the project. It believes such zones will ghetto-ise the tourists, but will also, by turning families off the land, create new migration and economic problems by forcing those affected to move to urban areas.

Global initiatives

Hoteliers are another group within the tourism circle which has recently been targeted to accept more responsibility for the environment in their everyday practice. One scheme is the International Hotels Environment Initiative, launched by the Prince of Wales in the summer of 1993. This was started by a group of international hoteliers, who felt a mechanism was needed for the better networking of environmental information. All members – some 7,500 hotels are now involved – receive a bulky manual, which represents the industry's guide to good practice, and covers topics such as waste management, energy and water conservation, noise, pesticides and herbicides, hazardous materials, and much else. The manual is also full of case studies, showing how hotels have been able to make savings by thinking more environmentally. The most famous of these is the London Hilton's idea of putting a brick in the cistern of each bathroom in the hotel, thus saving around 1.3 litres per flush.

The underlying assumption of an initiative that has clearly made a firm impact on the hotel trade is that good environmental practice makes business sense. But John Van Praag, the former chief executive of InterContinental Hotels, recently sounded a warning note about people's motives for embracing the idea: 'Being seen as environmentally sensitive is commercially very advantageous. I think it is a terrible motivation, however. If it is a side-product, great. But if we can't find it in our hearts to see the long-term importance of sustainability in our own industry, then there is something wrong with us.'[3]

The most recent initiative aimed at getting the world's tourism industry to be more environmentally aware is the Green Globe programme, launched in the summer of 1994 by the World Travel and Tourism Council Environment Research Centre. The aim is to get companies to commit themselves to undertake environmental improvements, after which they can receive advice, support and training, and be eligible for achievement awards. Andrew Blaza, director of the centre, says it would be easy but wrong to dismiss the initiative as a public-relations exercise. 'It's a very significant development,' he says. 'It's not just another charter, with plaques on the wall and nothing further being done. A lot of those raise awareness, but then leave a vacuum behind. This programme is different, it provides all the resources a company needs to fulfil its commitment to environmental improvement.'[4]

Good for business

As business generally in the UK has started to become more aware of and sensitive to environmental issues, so the tourism industry has begun to recognise the need to move in a similar direction. But progress has been painfully slow: many look at sustainability in very narrow terms, and avoid the more fundamental issues that might challenge the view that they should be allowed to expand indefinitely.

Too many tour operators, both big and small, still ignore or are unconvinced by the argument that to take up the sustainable tourism idea not only demonstrates a responsible attitude to the environment, but also can make sense in commercial terms. This argument is based on the belief that the expectations of tourists are gradually changing, and that many people are now prepared to pay more for an experience they feel will be less destructive of the environment, and more in line with the principles of sustainable tourism.

These changing attitudes have also raised the question of whether the tourist industry, and indeed tourists themselves, should be contributing towards the cost of maintaining and repairing the physical environment, on the principle that 'the polluter pays'. In several parts of the country, different methods are being considered or tested of raising money for

Down on a Staffordshire farm. Many farmers are now turning to tourism to save their businesses.

funding specific conservation projects.

During the 1990s several UK tourism and countryside agencies have been making efforts to persuade the tourist industry of the wisdom of adopting a sustainable approach. The *Green Light* booklet, produced jointly by the Countryside Commission, the English Tourist Board and the Rural Development Commission, puts over a message that 'it pays to go green'. The authors list the practical benefits to be gained from such a change:

- Increased competitiveness, raised quality and a better position in the market.
- Greater overall efficiency.
- Improved image, credibility, and a better basis for growth.
- Lower raw material and waste disposal costs.
- A better working environment for staff, and a higher quality environment for local communities.
- Opportunities for developing new services and products.[5]

One direct outcome of the booklet has been the South Devon Green Tourism Initiative (GTI), set up in 1992 as a pilot project to see how the principles of sustainable tourism could best be explained and put into practice. One of its main aims is to encourage good practice amongst local tourism businesses and operators. With this in mind Paul Dingle, the project manager, has devised a Green Audit Kit. 'What business would reject a strategy that reduced its costs, improved the quality of its services and secured its long-term future?' runs its bold introduction. Its aim is to help businesses, by the awarding of 'greenie points', to understand and control the impacts they make on the environment and to adjust their policies accordingly.

During the first year of the initiative 65 businesses, including tourist attractions such as Paignton Zoo and the Plymouth Dome, as well as large and small hotels, invested in the kit. Alongside it, a subsidised environmental audit service was made available, although take-up on this has been slow. 'The tourism businesses in the area aren't yet ready,' Paul Dingle says. 'The notion of having to pay for an audit is still fairly alien, and must be nurtured through the kit and through training.'[6] He is also working on an idea for identifying goods at Cash and Carry stores used by accommodation providers with a Green Audit Kit logo, to promote 'greener goods'.

In a very different landscape, the North Pennines Tourism Partnership is also working to promote sustainable principles and practice. Described as 'England's Last Wilderness', this upland area, once the wealthiest lead-mining centre in Europe, is one of the most remote. The partnership is aiming to show that conservation and rural development can be mutually supportive. It's putting an emphasis on strengthening the rural economy, by helping small tourism businesses to improve their effectiveness while remaining environmentally responsible. One result of its work has been the formation of a tourism association, which has helped to break down the isolation of many businesses in the area.

Such initiatives are not confined to rural areas. In Eastleigh, a largely urban area of Hampshire, a Green Tourism Unit was set up by the district council. It has produced 'green' plans for hotels, carried out environmental audits free of charge, and helped businesses obtain grants for environmental projects. Much of the work has been on small, very practical matters, such as advising businesses on aspects of tree planting. One hotel was encouraged to plant an orchard in its grounds, to the benefit both of its guests and the local wildlife. Some hotel operators have been encouraged to target members of conservation groups, offering them packages that have a 'green' theme.

One increasingly popular way of encouraging the tourism industry to think in more sustainable terms is to set up an awards scheme. One of the first to be established was the Tourism for Tomorrow awards, set up in 1990 by the Federation of Tour Operators and the British Tourist Authority, and run by British Airways. Originally directed at tour operators and the resorts they targeted, the awards are now open to a wide range of tourism businesses from all over the world, and are given to those which can show evidence of environmentally responsible management.

Within the UK the idea is now spreading at local level, with award schemes established in Cornwall, Devon and the North Pennines. For the South Devon GTI, a green charter awards scheme was considered, but rejected on the grounds that, according to Paul Dingle, such charters are 'simply a convenient way of businesses promoting an environmental image without actually doing anything'. The project has plumped instead for a more stringent two-tier green tourism awards scheme, for which businesses have to show they have taken real steps to improve their environmental performance and management.

Back to the Wilderness: France

A former wilderness area in western France, which now attracts about a million visitors a year, is to be cleared of buildings and restored to its former state, after twenty years of campaigning by environmentalists.

At peak periods thousands of cars pour on to the site of La Pointe de Raz, a Breton beauty spot at the tip of Cap Sizun in Finistère, or tour the adjoining Baie des Trepasses. Now the area is to be cleared of commerce, following local government approval of plans to demolish a shopping centre, hotels, a car park, and other buildings that have sprung up since the Second World War.

It has taken five years to buy up the land from more than a thousand owners, on what is now designated a *grand site national*. When work is completed cars will be banned from the site; instead visitors will have to take a special bus.

The industry pays

Changing attitudes within the industry have led to several schemes designed to raise money from the tourism industry itself – usually by appealing to its self-interest. On the Lizard Peninsula in Cornwall, for example, local holiday-park owners who depend for their livelihood on the beach at Kennack Sands have been persuaded to part-fund a facelift for the collapsing sea wall, as a first step to improving the appearance of the beach and improving access. Dave Lewis, the Lizard Project officer, says: 'In developing support from the industry the key to success has been the establishment of a sense of ownership of the measures to improve the quality of the local environment. The industry is also quick to realise the marketing potential of its support for a quality environment.'[7]

In Cumbria, conservation work that repairs damage done by visitors to the upland parts of the county has been part-funded by the Cumbrian

Tourist Board, which has asked all its 1,500 commercial members to pledge a sum towards the work each year. Tourism businesses are also contributing to an environmental fund as part of the West Country's 'Celebrate the Countryside' sustainable tourism initiative. By paying £45 into the fund, and agreeing to a green charter, they become members of a green card scheme. This puts them in touch with interested potential customers, who sign up to receive a quarterly newsletter. The fund is used for projects such as repairing footpaths, waymarking nature trails, improving access for disabled people, or supporting the work of local conservation organisations. By 1994 some 2,500 members of the general public and 30 trade members had signed up for the scheme.

The tourist pays

The idea of getting tourists to pay their bit towards the cost of keeping the environment they are visiting in good shape would seem to be fraught with difficulties. The most obvious is people's reluctance to pay for anything that was previously free, particularly if it is a question of access to an area of countryside. Ideas such as a tourism tax, which operates in a number of countries, generally arouse hostility in the UK. Yet the various charging schemes now being tried out have produced a surprisingly positive response.

One method of raising quite substantial sums of money is by adding a supplement to the cost of a meal or accommodation. This has been done for example by a hotelier based south of Dartmoor, who put a 25p (1%) levy on the cost of an evening meal. The idea raised some £1,200 annually over a three-year period, during which only one guest asked not to pay. The money has been used for projects undertaken by the Devon Wildlife Trust, which originally made the suggestion to the hotel.

On the Isle of Skye in Scotland, the owner of a mountaineering school in Strathcarron put a £10 conservation levy on the bill of all his customers, and last year raised £2,200 for footpath restoration. The Countrywide Holidays Association charges its guests an extra £1 per week, which is then put into an environmental fund used for conservation projects. A similar scheme is now being considered by some of the providers of accommodation involved with the Tarka Project. (See case study, page 49.)

Another method is to put a levy on the use of car parks, with the money being designated for conservation work. An example of this is a Footpaths Fund recently launched in the Peak District. In some places 'honesty boxes' have been placed in car parks, inviting voluntary contributions. One idea being tested by the South Devon GTI is a discount voucher scheme. Visitors buy a book of vouchers, which gives them discounts on a range of tourism 'products', that in total add up to more than the price of the book. Traders and operators benefit overall because of the increased publicity and trade, while the money collected from the sale of the books is used for conservation projects, such as footpath maintenance. The scheme has been successful enough to warrant being extended throughout the county.

One of the more recent schemes designed to help people raise money for such purposes is that of a local tourism heritage trust, under a scheme run by the Countryside Commission and the English Tourist Board. A trust is created by a group of local businesses, each of which raises money in its own way, invites bids from conservation bodies or projects once a year, and then allocates the funds. The Peak Tourism Partnership and the North Pennines Tourism Partnership are among those taking part in pilot projects. Others are in progress in Devon, Humberside, Lancashire and Kent.

The growth of these schemes, and the fact that they're proving viable with both the public and the tourism industry, suggests there is still plenty of scope for tapping into people's real concern for the protection and conservation of the coast and countryside.

Light on the Land

Northern Ireland

Twenty-five years of The Troubles have, paradoxically, put Northern Ireland in a better position than any other part of the UK to adopt a sustainable approach to tourism.

The pressures created by tourists have been considerably fewer than those elsewhere, while the rural areas which make up most of the country remain relatively untouched and underdeveloped. Today, while the potential for tourism to help with economic regeneration is increasingly being recognised, there's also a growing awareness of the need to protect the physical environment and local culture, and to involve communities in developing appropriate tourism initiatives. These circumstances, together with the strong community feeling in rural areas, make it possible that the sustainable approach now being encouraged by tourist and government agencies and tested in several areas will gain ground.

The province is not short of tourists. The number of foreign visitors travelling to Northern Ireland is in fact higher than it was when The Troubles began: in 1993 it was 1.26 million, compared with 435,000 at the lowest point. But large numbers of these visitors went on business, or to see friends and relatives. The number visiting for a holiday was only 251,000, whereas in 1968 before The Troubles began it was 378,000.

The negative image created by the unceasing political conflict has clearly deterred many people from making a pleasure trip to the province – especially from Britain, which supplied half the visitors in 1993, but only a quarter of those taking a holiday there. Yet many who do take the tourist trail are surprised and taken aback by the immense variety of

The Giant's Causeway in County Antrim.

scenery on offer – from the mountains of Mourne to the loughs of Fermanagh, from the gloriously rugged Antrim coast to the Sperrin mountains in County Tyrone – as well as by the diversity of the country's historic sites and other attractions.

Yet the province is certainly not a trouble-free zone as far as tourism is concerned. Day trippers from towns in the eastern part of the country are exerting increasing pressure on resorts such as Bangor, Newcastle and Portrush, while elsewhere on the coast many fragile areas are threatened with over-use. There are also plenty of examples of inappropriate development, including a huge growth in stationary caravans; of a lack of respect for vernacular buildings; and of poor management that has failed to prevent the environment from deteriorating.

These problems and others eventually led the Northern Ireland Tourist Board (NITB) to take a hard look at the question of sustainable tourism. In 1993 it published the report *Tourism in Northern Ireland: A Sustainable Approach*. This outlined the principles of sustainable tourism, showing how it could benefit the environment, the industry, the community and the visitor. It provided a detailed guide for anyone running a tourism operation, showing the practical steps that needed to be taken to achieve a sustainable practice. It also attempted to counter some widely held misconceptions: 'Sustainable tourism is not a narrow specialist niche market, but an attitude and approach which influences all aspects of tourism for the good,' it stated. 'It is a tourism which respects the environment and operates within the tolerance of the people who live here, a tourism which is light on the land – a long-term tourism.'

This kind of thinking was subsequently reflected in the NITB's new tourism development strategy, formulated to provide a blueprint for the remaining years of the century. The final version was published in the autumn of 1994, after a period of consultation which led to the strategy being underpinned even more firmly by sustainable principles. The main development priorities were seen as relating tourism to the environment; involving the local community; the need to aim for quality; and the importance of all parties working together.

Other bodies have also been developing strategies based on sustainable principles. The National Trust, which owns 12% of all the attractions in the province, devised a five-year tourism development plan which was influenced by the NITB's exercise. Part of its plans are to shift the tourism emphasis from the more pressurised north and east, especially the coastal areas, to the west and south.

Some elements of the NITB's strategy can also be found in some of the initiatives that have recently got off the ground in the province. One which many see as an excellent model is the Fermanagh Tourism Strategic Development Initiative (see page 128). Here, and in many other rural regions of Northern Ireland, the sustainability emphasis is as much an economic as an environmental one, with tourism development and community development intertwined.

South Armagh is one of the areas where regeneration is high on the agenda. The many community projects being developed there aim to restore local self-confidence by providing a much-needed boost to the local economy through the creation of new businesses and jobs. Many of these have a tourism component or base, with one of the main aims being to rid the region of its 'bandit country' image.

One of these tourism-based projects has been initiated by local farmers belonging to the Ring of Gullion Rural Tourism Group. Like many in Northern Ireland, they're facing a decline in their business, and want to explore the potential for tourism. In order to provide additional income and create fresh jobs, they've established a horse/pony trekking trail using traditional bridal paths, and provided accommodation for visitors.

Another community-based project in this Area of Outstanding Natural Beauty is a new environmental/tourism centre, set up by the Slieve Gullion Courtyard Development Group. In this case old farm buildings have been renovated to create a centre which will cater for school children on both sides of the border, provide work-space units and, eventually, self-catering accommodation.

While areas such as South Armagh are pushing to increase the number of visitors in such ways, in other places one of the main issues is how to manage large numbers of them. In the Mountains of Mourne in County Down, another Area of Outstanding Natural Beauty, and one that's within easy reach of most of Northern Ireland's population, there's the usual problem of footpath erosion, as well as that of illegal dumping. These are just two of the many concerns that have prompted the NITB and the Department of the Environment to initiate a new visitor and environmental strategy for the area, which will aim to safeguard and improve the landscape while enhancing people's enjoyment of it.

Another very popular attraction is the Giant's Causeway in County Antrim, a World Heritage Site and National Nature Reserve, which attracts 370,000 visitors from more than fifty countries, eager to see its extraordinary volcanic rock formations. Fortunately fewer than 10% of the visitors explore the entire site, with its dramatic cliffs and headlands;

but even this is enough to cause considerable damage. At present visitors are being kept off sections of the cliff path because of landslides, and its permanent closure is now being considered by the National Trust, which owns the site.

Controlling the movement of visitors without spoiling their enjoyment of the attraction is a tricky balancing act. Restricting them to certain paths or areas is one measure that is being adopted. This is what the National Trust has done at Portstewart Strand in Derry, one of the finest areas of beach and sand dunes along the coastline, which is used for a variety of recreational activities. Serious erosion caused by trampling feet has resulted in the creation of 'blowouts' – large hollows of bare sand – which have required substantial repair work. The trust has marked out special paths around the dunes, but also zoned the beach area, so that visitors involved in motorised water sports are separated off from those who prefer bathing, surfing and angling.

This kind of visitor management is especially needed in the more fragile environments. These include the many nature reserves established to provide for recreation while simultaneously protecting the rarer habitats, vegetation and wildlife. Two such reserves are in the Peatlands Park near Portadown in Armagh, just south of Lough Neagh, where many unusual plant and insect species are to be found within the peatlands. Access to these areas is restricted to the use of a network of board walks that cross the woods, the open bogs and the two nature reserves.

Managing visitors effectively should also include providing them with sensitive and appropriate interpretation. Peatlands Park is seen as an example of good practice here, as is the Lough Neagh Discovery Centre a few miles north, in the Oxford Island National Nature Reserve. The centre provides interpretation of the ecology of the lough by means of audio-visual shows, computer simulations and interactive displays. These are supplemented by guided activities around the reserve, designed to increase visitors' environmental awareness, and include birdwatching, boat trips, pond dipping, and the exploration of nature walks and trails.

Visitor centres can do a good job in interpreting an attraction for visitors, but they can also arouse controversy. Great care needs to be taken over their design and positioning if they are not to become yet another inappropriate development and an intrusion on the landscape. This was one of several issues that came up during the development of the £4 million interpretative centre at Navan Fort near the city of Armagh, which eventually opened in 1993.

Navan, the ancient seat of Ulster's kings as well as one of the most important archaeological sites in Western Europe, has been compared in importance to Stonehenge or the Parthenon. The original siting of the visitor centre, close to the ancient mound itself, was widely seen as intrusive. In the face of intense criticism, the project directors agreed to move the building further away from the mound, and to think again about its relationship with the landscape. There it stands today, discreetly folded into a hillside half a mile from the fort, cleverly blended into the countryside, its circular design echoing the shape of the fort itself.

The explanatory material on display at Navan also caused dis-agreements about the interpretation of Celtic myths and history. Culture, language and politics remain interwined in Northern Ireland, with South Armagh being one of the regions with a strong linguistic heritage in Irish. Sharing this heritage with visitors is seen as a good way of preserving and developing it. This is a key element in the thinking behind the proposal for a new cultural activity centre at Mullaghbawn, near Newry, put together by the Slieve Gullion Cultural Centre Working Group. The aim is for the building to be a centre for the study and development of Irish language and literature, music, song, dance, storytelling and drama, which will be shared by the community and visitors to the area through a programme of courses and events. The idea is to provide accommodation in the centre for visitors taking part in the longer courses.

The Irish language is also an important element in a rural regeneration initiative in the Creggan area of County Tyrone, situated in the foothills of the Sperrin mountains. It includes the development of a traditional farm settlement, owned by one of the last Gaelic speakers in the area, into self-catering cottages designed to reflect the traditional village settlements of Creggan. A nearby visitor centre provides a history of an area rich in archaeological features, as well as offering traditional music, song, dance and storytelling.

This project is one of several funded under the European Community's

LEADER programme, which supports innovative economic development projects driven by local communities in areas of rural disadvantage. The programme has provided £4 million for Northern Ireland over the last three years, and a further round of funding is about to begin. There is some feeling that there has been an over-reliance on history in many projects funded during the first phase, and that Brussels is now looking for more innovation, and less imitation. Such support is vital for many rural communities, where the main hope for regeneration is now widely felt to lie with tourism.

European money has also been secured to help fund some cross-border tourism programmes, announced by the government in the autumn of 1994 in the wake of the paramilitary ceasefires. While there had been increasing cooperation in recent times between the tourist boards on both sides of the border, this was clearly a major step forward in their efforts to market Ireland as a whole.

Fermanagh Tourism Strategic Development Initiative

Lakeland Country Breaks is an initiative designed to attract visitors into the rural lakelands of County Fermanagh for weekend breaks devised, agreed and organised by the communities themselves. The scheme, which is currently being piloted in six villages, is based on the Country Village Breaks idea originated in Herefordshire ten years ago by David Gorvett (see page 135), and subsequently developed in Wales.

Within the county of Fermanagh, where 70% of the population live in rural areas, tourism is the second most important element in the local economy, accounting for around 22% of local employment. There's also a large number of organisations and interest groups active at community level, many involved in schemes for the economic and social regeneration of their areas, and the preservation and celebration of their culture through festivals and other events. This set of circumstances appears to provide fertile ground for an initiative that, if successful, could act as a model for communities in other parts of the province.

The scheme emerged from a larger tourism initiative set up by Fermanagh District Council, part of which led to thirty representatives from community interest groups in the county visiting a variety of economic development, tourism, cultural and community projects in Wales. The group was particularly impressed by the Welsh Country Village Breaks project, and decided it was a good model for an experiment in rural tourism in its own area. The scheme had a number of objectives, including:

- Spreading the benefits of tourism to the most underdeveloped areas in the county;
- Protecting the more sensitive areas by providing an experience for visitors in other areas
- Creating and maintaining new jobs with a minimum of capital investment;
- Enabling groups to coordinate the marketing of their areas;
- Raising the status, confidence and profile of the local community.

The pilot stage of the scheme finally got under way in 1994, with the involvement of the villages of Belcoo, Derrygonnelly, Ederney, Garrison, Irvinestown and Manorhamilton. The activities on offer included walking, visiting local historic sites, pony trekking, water skiing, fishing, caving, windsurfing and boat trips.

However, the project experienced an initial setback when, despite considerable interest, bookings proved to be very slow. Price appeared to be the sticking point, so this was lowered from £85 to £65 a person. There is now greater confidence that the scheme will take off when it begins properly in the new season.

Aideen McGinley, Fermanagh's director of development, stresses the grassroots nature of the initiative. 'It would not have reached the stage it is at so successfully if all the pre-development work, the sharing of experience, training and hand-holding had not taken place,' she says. About the possibility of the scheme being copied elsewhere she is cautious: 'I am not naive enough to think that these ideal conditions, which were created over a long period of time and now exist in Fermanagh, are to be found so readily elsewhere. In many councils, rural and community development are at arm's-length from tourism, if indeed they exist at all as separate functions.'

8 Acting Locally

'A stranger is a friend you have yet to meet.'

Traditional Irish saying

Much of the damage created by mass tourism has come about through the exploitation of people and places by outsiders. Whether they work for governments, developers, large companies or tourism businesses, they have, in their desire to promote tourism or make money, taken little or no heed of the needs or wishes of local people.

The consequences have been nothing short of disastrous for some communities. Their natural resources have been plundered, their traditional way of life destroyed, their culture repackaged and trivialised to cater for the 'needs' of tourists. The result has been a steady move towards uniformity, and a huge loss of that distinctiveness which makes particular places and countries attractive to visitors.

Of course local people often collude in such a process, especially in poor communities where the offer of a job in a tourist development, even if it's merely a seasonal one, can be very attractive. In recent years, however, local groups and individuals have been fighting back, sometimes with success. One of the results has been a greater awareness of the value of involving the local community in the planning and carrying out of tourism developments. There's also a growing realisation that, if tourism is to be sustainable, it needs to be seen in positive terms by local people, and to respect their local arts, culture and language. It's also beginning to be recognised that tourism should bring local people real financial benefits: all too often it's outside companies, both national and multinational, and other entrepreneurs which end up taking the bulk of the tourists' money.

The Golowan Band at Penzance Mazey Day, Cornwall 1993. The talents of musicians, dancers, actors and storytellers are being used to attract tourists in many rural areas.

Local involvement

Within the UK there is a growing realisation that if sustainable tourism is to be the goal, then the support of local people is critical. They more than anyone else have a vested interest in preventing their locality being damaged by tourism. They can also turn out to be the best guardians of the physical environment in their area. Of course, such an interest can easily shade into the 'Not-In-My-Back-Yard' (NIMBY) syndrome, where self-interest is often allied to resistance to any change at all. Consultation on a planned tourism development needs to be with all groups in a community, not just with a few articulate or well-known individuals.

Many of the recent projects or initiatives designed to promote and manage tourism in a sustainable way in the countryside have looked for ways of involving the local community from an early stage. A good example of this was to be found recently in Berwick-upon-Tweed in Northumberland, an area containing the mountainous Cheviot and Kyloe Hills, the valley of the River Tweed, and many miles of sandy coastline. Research by the Rural Tourism Development Project at Bristol University prompted a decision in 1990 by Berwick council to develop a sustainable tourism strategy for the whole area. Public meetings were held in all the main towns and villages to outline the main options for development, and to gather local views. A draft plan was then sent out for comment, followed by a series of 'teach-ins', before the strategy was finally approved by the local borough council. The result was broadly welcomed by local people.

According to Bernard Lane, director of the Bristol project, the moral of the story is clear. 'The first lesson to draw is that sustainable tourism strategies can be developed in participation with communities and the tourist industry. It is a slow and sometimes difficult task, but it can be done.' He also believes the consultations were real, and not a public relations exercise. 'The initial meetings were often long, sometimes noisy, but always useful. They were open, but carefully structured to help communities to begin to consider in detail where their futures lay. They were the beginning of a dialogue.'[1]

The creation of the new National Forest in Derbyshire, Leicestershire and Staffordshire has also involved a wide-ranging consultation exercise. Some 17,000 copies of a draft strategy were distributed in supermarkets, leisure centres, libraries, schools, and from stalls in shopping centres, and meetings were held in local villages. A questionnaire inviting comments elicited 1,200 responses, and more than two hundred people wrote in with comments.

'The response exceeded all our expectations,' says Simon Evans, who is preparing the final strategy for the forest. 'People have helped us to sharpen up the document, and have highlighted some notable omissions, especially over issues such as community involvement, education, and the potential role of the arts.'[2] Public anxieties focused on the amount of traffic that would come into the forest; on the protection of existing wildlife areas as well as the creation of new ones; and on the need for facilities for noisy water sports to be appropriately sited so as not to be intrusive. There was also widespread concern that the government would fail to provide the money that would allow such an imaginative plan to be implemented.

Local involvement is of course important not only when planning a tourist development, but also when dealing with problems caused by existing ones. On the Lizard Peninsula in Cornwall, the growing number of sub-aqua divers has recently been creating a problem for local residents and other beach users. Access roads were being blocked, cars and trailers were stuck on the beach, speed restrictions were being ignored, and the noise was becoming excessive. At the instigation of the Lizard Peninsular Project, a meeting was held between local people, the divers and the British Sub-Aqua Club. The outcome was a positive one: a code of conduct was agreed, as was a voluntary speed limit for boats. An annual meeting was established to review the success of the code, and look at any further problems that arose.

The rural forum

In a few places a more permanent structure, generally known as a rural tourism development forum, has been set up. This gives local people the chance not just to respond to other people's plans, but to discuss and develop their own initiatives, and look at ways in which they can help the local economy while conserving their environmental and cultural assets. It allows them to encourage and promote small-scale tourism, making good use of their specialist knowledge, while ensuring that control effectively remains in their hands.

Among the earliest to be established was the Brit Valley Forum in Dorset, one of several generated by the work of the Bristol Rural Tourism Development Project. Based on Beaminster and ten surrounding villages, the forum has prompted or been involved with several initiatives. These include the conversion of old farm buildings into crafts workshops, the regeneration of a disused water mill, the creation of circular walks and church trails, and the production of a brochure detailing the history and attractions of and local accommodation in Dorset's 'Hidden Valley'.

A forum has been established in other areas, in the Staffordshire Moorlands, Shropshire, Hertfordshire, Durham, Wiltshire and the Forest of Dean. One of the most successful, now in its ninth year, has been in Dulverton, a small and remote Somerset town within the Exmoor National Park, which has suffered economic decline in recent years. The forum, which consists of accommodation providers, shopkeepers and others, has sought to attract visitors by producing an annual leaflet about the town, staging exhibitions on historical themes, organising a sculpture residency, and bringing in arts performers. Its biggest achievement has been to secure the £300,000 needed to turn some disused or under-used historic buildings into a heritage and information centre and gallery.

The group is now linking up with nine similar communities in countries such as Chile and Tanzania, sharing information on how to manage tourism at local level. 'Nothing succeeds like success,' says Jan Ross, a long-standing forum member. 'We used to feel before that the authorities were making all the decisions. Now we feel we have a voice. It provides a good opportunity for people to air their ideas, however mad, without the dictates of the council. It's given people a feeling of empowerment.'[3]

Getting together

Cooperation between local people with a common interest in developing tourism in a sustainable fashion has been a feature of these and other initiatives. One of the most imaginative and initially successful local ventures has been the Country Village Weekend Breaks scheme. Started by David Gorvett in the Herefordshire village of Eardisley in 1985, it subsequently embraced other villages in the area, and in Staffordshire and Cumbria, and now has parallel operations in Wales and Ireland (see page 128). The idea involves a small group of visitors, generally between four and fourteen in number, spending a weekend as guests of a village. They stay in local people's houses, eat local food, go on visits to churches, farms and pubs, take part in guided walks around the area, and observe craft and music demonstrations.

The recession has hit the scheme badly in the last two years, partly because it appeals mainly to the over-50 age-group, whose income has been particularly squeezed. Many potential visitors are now foregoing such short breaks in order to make sure they can afford their main holiday. As a result, visitors come almost entirely from overseas, notably North America and Japan. The scheme has been difficult to market, and in England is now confined to a few villages around Eardisley. A further obstacle has been the turnover of providers: in some villages key people have moved, or gone bankrupt. However some villages have withdrawn for more positive reasons, having developed their facilities to a level where they no longer need such a crutch.

David Gorvett believes the scheme has produced some useful spin-offs in Herefordshire, including a number of publications detailing local walks, and a greater knowledge of the county overseas. This in turn has led to a slow improvement in facilities, and greater confidence on the part of the providers in meeting the needs of visitors. But he also recognises the need for outside support: 'The idea is now generally accepted in the area because it has been seen to work,' he says. 'But it's become obvious to me that, although a venture like ours in sustainable rural tourism is a lovely idea, it needs to be incorporated within a wider strategy if it is to survive in the turbulent ocean of market forces.'[4]

Local products
Helping to sustain the local economy is an important feature of this kind of small-scale initiative: the more visitors that can be persuaded to buy local goods and services, the better it is for the area. In many areas

efforts are now being made to market such goods and services in a way that makes it easy for visitors to know where they can get hold of them.

Such a promotion is linked to specifically local produce, as in the case of the initiative of the North Pennines Tourism Partnership. The project has published a Produce Trail leaflet, with details of local goods that can be bought in the area, and a map showing where to buy them. It includes food 'grown, ground and made locally', such as Alston Cheese or Cumberland Mustard, as well as information on places to buy local crafts and clothing. Crafts are also the focus of a similar initiative in the Yorkshire Dales, where businesses involved with making candles, glass, jewellery, sculpture, pottery and furniture have combined to produce a Dales Country Workshop Trail leaflet, which is mailed to all places that accommodate visitors. A similar leaflet has been produced to encourage visitors to buy from local crafts people, food producers and retailers around the Peak District National Park.

A thematic approach has sometimes proved successful in promoting a local area and at the same time bringing in much-needed revenue. The Big Apple Festival, which takes place in an undeveloped apple-growing region in Herefordshire, is just such a community event. On four weekends a year, during spring and autumn, a series of experiences linked by the apple theme are laid on, including orchard walks, displays, apple teas, cooking demonstrations, cider tasting, apple identification and farm visits. Apart from attracting new visitors to the area, some of whom then stay on in local bed and breakfast accommodation, the festival has helped to raise funds for many local groups that form the backbone of life in the parishes concerned.

Another way of supporting local production while encouraging a sustainable approach has been found in Devon, where members of the recently formed Tarka Country Tourist Association have to sign a 'green charter'. This, among other commitments, pledges them to favour local products when catering for visitors. The association is a good example of a grassroots initiative in which providers of accommodation – in this case in small hotels and farmhouses – have been able to create a network through which they can adopt a more sustainable approach to their dealings with visitors. (See case study, page 49).

Getting Personal: Senegal

In the Lower Casamance region of Senegal in Africa, a 'Tourism for Discovery' project is fostering more personal relationships between tourists and local people, by ensuring that the visitor is treated as a guest rather than an intruder.

Tourists, whose numbers are strictly controlled, are put up in simple lodgings that are built, operated and managed by the villagers. Access is by bush taxi or canoe. There are nature excursions, and informal talks by villagers on their history and culture. Tourists are even encouraged to help with agricultural and construction work.

Most food and supplies are produced locally, and meals are prepared using traditional recipes. The scheme has given a boost to the local economy. Returns are immediate, and the profits generated have helped both to create new jobs, and enhance educational and health facilities in the villages.

Down on the farm

Across the country generally, farmers are joining forces locally to promote the facilities they can offer to tourists. An increasing number are now diversifying into providing bed and breakfast accommodation, opening the farms up as tourist attractions or, in some cases, selling the land off for commercial leisure use.

Recent changes in agricultural policies, both in Britain and in Europe, have forced many farmers to move away from depending on food production, and to look for alternative sources of income. In some cases they've seen this as the only way of being able to stay on the land and remain in business. If they're forced to sell up, there's a danger of their land being used for inappropriate development. In choosing to visit or stay on a farm, visitors are thus helping to maintain the working life of the countryside, and its diversity and distinctiveness.

There's nothing new about farm holidays, but in recent years they've enjoyed a growing popularity. Around 35,000 farms in the UK now provide accommodation and catering services. In the West Country farm-based tourism provides almost a quarter of farm income. One survey showed that in 1991 24% of farms in England and Wales were involved in at least one tourism enterprise. In Cumbria alone it's estimated that 1,200 farmers are now offering accommodation to visitors.

Recent research shows that while only 9% of the British population has stayed on a farm in the last three years, 45% say they are attracted to the idea of doing so. The factors people consider most important in making such a choice are the farm's country setting, its peace and quiet, the affordable price, and – almost as important – the quality of the breakfast. Such visits clearly have a special appeal for families with children, for whom a stay on a farm is widely seen as a rewarding and educative experience, with a good variety of things for them to see, touch and do.[5]

Under the umbrella of the Farm Holiday Bureau, there are now 88 farm holiday groups around the UK, marketing the holidays on offer in their area, and passing on customers by word of mouth. Farm attractions are also growing in number. Some farmers are moving on from simply providing accommodation to setting up farm trails, devising interpretation for the surrounding land, or initiating weekend breaks based on outings to look at the local wildlife. They're now being helped to do this nationally by the Farm Holiday Bureau, which is developing new courses in farm and countryside interpretation. In some areas advice, training and financial assistance are being offered, as in the case of the Cumbria Farm Tourism initiative, set up in 1993. In Cornwall, farm tourism workshops are shortly to be offered by Project Explore.

Sustaining the arts

The arts are an important element in tourism. The most recent national figures show that arts-related tourism spending was worth £3.1 billion to the UK economy, and accounted for 25% of all tourist spending.[6] A very large proportion of this is of course spent in towns and cities. But arts initiatives of different kinds are increasingly appearing in rural areas, many now specifically aimed at visitors as well as local people.

Arts and crafts producers of all kinds and abilities – potters, painters, weavers, sculptors – choose to live and work in the countryside. Where there is an end-product involved, their work obviously contributes to the local economy, and is often included in the promotional literature for tourists which details local goods and services. More generally, their presence contributes to the diversity of life in rural areas, and can be used to help promote its cultural assets.

Some tourism initiatives are now making a point of including the arts in their plans. This may entail compiling a guide of the professional artists and craftspeople working in their area. A few are going further, and giving direct support to artists to enable them to work with or for tourists. In the North Pennines, for example, a textile artist has been in residence during the last year at the Allenheads Heritage Centre, helping both locals and visitors to learn how to work with textiles, and trying to find new opportunities for textile makers in the area to get their work seen and sold. The residency may be extended for a further year.

But the arts are also about performance. The talents of local actors, musicians and storytellers are beginning to be used to attract tourists into rural areas. Community plays, begun by playwright Ann Jellicoe in the West Country in the late 1970s, are now to be found all over the countryside, many based in villages. Part of the brief of the current Wiltshire Downs Project, for instance, is to develop access to and participation in the arts. Apart from compiling a register of local events, courses and venues, the project's efforts have been concentrated on developing a community play for the village of Cherhill, in conjunction with a local theatre company. The promenade production was staged in the summer of 1994 around the village, at Oldbury Castle, and at the famous white horse on the hillside.

Last year the people of Carradale, a fishing village on Kintyre in the Western Isles of Scotland, also used theatre as a way of telling the story of their community. As with Cherhill, a theatre company acted as the catalyst, being given the commission of bringing to life for visitors the interpretation of the village's history. The success of the resulting play, developed in conjunction with local people, led to the villagers themselves organising and leading a programme of events throughout the summer.[7]

The very distinctive culture of certain places has always been part of

Cultural Prostitution: Hawaii

In 1989 there were 5.75 million visitors to Hawaii; by the year 2010 it's predicted there will be 11.5 million. The dramatic development of tourism has radically affected the relationship of the local people to the land and sea, which lies at the root of their culture.

It has played a major role in the destruction of ancient Hawaiian burial grounds, significant archaeological sites and sacred places, as new hotels and other developments have been built over culturally significant sites.

Many Hawaiians are offended by the exploitation and packaging of their culture for economic benefit. The Reverend Kaleo Patterson, of the Hawaii Ecumenical Coalition of Tourism, says: 'The culture is romanticised to appeal to the exotic fantasies of world travellers. This perpetuates racist and sexist stereotypes that are culturally inappropriate and demeaning. The issue becomes one of cultural prostitution.'

their attraction to visitors. This is certainly true of Cornwall, with its strong tradition of storytelling based on the county's eventful maritime history. Project Explore, based in south-east Cornwall, has made imaginative use of the skills of local storytellers, by using them as interpreters to convey the history and culture of the region to visitors, as an alternative to more conventional methods such as leaflets, wayside panels and guide books.

Local people have also been heavily involved in another of the project's arts-based initiatives, the Festival of the Sea, held for the first time in 1993 in the medieval port of Looe and the traditional fishing village of Polperro. The festival was devised in order to get tourists to stay for longer in the villages, to raise the level of understanding of the fishing industry, and to increase visitors' awareness of the influence of the sea on the history and life of the area. Talks and walks, storytelling, and a wide range of activities made up the programme. The festival was judged a success: people had worked well together to put on an event that, despite appalling weather, proved attractive to tourists. It has now been decided to make the festival biennial.

All these initiatives, whether inspired and organised by a formal project or developed from the grassroots upwards, make use of the skills, resources and ideas of local people. Apart from the intrinsic value of involving them in such collective efforts, these initiatives also enable local people to keep a close eye and a measure of control on how tourism is developed in their area. They also make it rather more likely that any tourism developments will, in scale and nature, be in harmony with the landscape, and appropriate to the traditions and patterns of local people's lives.

Rural Connections

The Republic of Ireland

In the autumn of 1994 the Irish Tourist Board unfurled its strategy for tourism for the rest of the century. It made its fundamental aim and approach quite clear:

'We must develop a central image of Ireland as an uncrowded, relaxed island of great scenic beauty, with a distinctive heritage and culture, a friendly welcoming people, high-quality facilities, and a superb unspoilt environment for outoor activity. The key to securing a product which can live up to this image is to follow a policy of sustainable tourism.'

This description is not just another marketing ploy, for much of this image holds true in reality. But for how long will the label 'uncrowded' still be applicable? Seven years ago there were calls for the number of tourists to be doubled. In 1993 the country attracted 3.3 million a year, while the new strategy has set a target of increasing tourism revenue by 50% by the end of 1999.

Such attempts to increase the income from tourism are understandable in the circumstances. Ireland is a relatively sparsely populated country where unemployment is running high, at an average of 20% of the workforce. Rural communities are under threat as European Community agricultural subsidies decline. Yet, with funding support from Europe, 25,000 new jobs in tourism were created in the period 1988-1993, with a similar number expected to be generated in the next five years. In what is essentially a rural country, rural tourism – which constitutes some 60% of all tourism in Ireland – is now being seen as one of the prime means of regenerating local communities.

Happily, Ireland has been spared the worst effects of mass tourism,

A standing stone in Poulnabrone Dolmen, County Clare.

though it's recognised that this is more by accident than design. Nevertheless, the country has its pressure points at peak times of the year, with Dublin, Galway, Killarney and the Blarney Stone being the main honeypots. There can also be considerable pressure of numbers along the west coast in parts of Clare, Cork, Donegal, Kerry and Mayo; and in areas covered by some of the national parks, such as Glenveagh in Donegal and the Wicklow Uplands (see case study, page 147). The country also has its share of inappropriate development, much of which has skirted round the planning system. Bungalows are now threatening many of the finest coastal areas. Golf courses are one of the main growth industries, although there's generally enough space for these to be absorbed. There is also a substantial threat to fishing, one of the greatest attractions for tourists, because of pollution, poaching and disease.

The present drive to develop rural tourism is based on the belief that Ireland is particularly well placed to cater for the increasing number of people looking to get off the beaten track away from the mass of tourists, to get to know a small area intimately, and make real connections with local people. Yet while this assessment may be accurate, there are still many difficulties facing groups and individuals trying to develop rural tourism, as Marie O'Donald of the Irish Tourist Board admits:

'There's been an appalling slide away from the countryside, to the cities and overseas,' she says. 'So the rural infrastructure is poor, and there's a lack of tourism development. It's also hard for people to find matching funds for new projects. One of the main difficulties is creating a dynamic within a community that not only enables them to work together on a development, but to keep it together. It can take years for that to grow.'

Nevertheless, there are now a great number of small-scale tourism initiatives spread around the Irish countryside, run by cooperatives or community development associations. One of the longest established is the Ballyhoura Failte Society, a tourism cooperative working in the region where the counties of Cork, Limerick and Tipperary meet.

Here, in an area previously neglected by tourists, local people first got together in 1986, working with 'a five-year plan and a twenty-five year vision' to attract more visitors. Beginning in a modest way with agricultural study tours, the group was then selected for an EC agri-tourism pilot project, involving marketing Irish Country Holidays in Germany. Since then it has gradually built up a wide range of facilities and attractions: farm visits, cycle routes, horse riding, an outdoor pursuits centre, walks and trails in a mountain park, an English as a Foreign Language school, and much else. It's been a matter of all sections of the community planning and working together – voluntary groups, local businesses, the statutory services and private individuals. Joint marketing has also been a key element, as has the training in hospitality skills for those providing accommodation for visitors.

The result of all this effort has been a significant increase in tourism in 'Ballyhoura Country' – £1.1 million extra revenue between 1989 and 1992 – and the creation of many new jobs. One notable initiative has been the concerted attempt to improve the quality of the local restaurants. Each was subjected to an audit focussing on the quality of the food, the service, the environment and the management, with only those which reached the necessary standard on all four counts being included in a restaurant directory. Ten of those in the 1994 edition were new businesses; and over the past two years large-scale investment in improvements to restaurants has created fifty new jobs in this sector alone.

Many of these rural tourism projects are dependent on money from the European Community. They are generally underpinned by sustainable principles – although some of the larger EC projects have caused controversy by not consulting local people, for instance before establishing visitor centres.

One of the most recent projects to be funded by the EC is in the Brandon Mountain area in County Kerry, a glacial landscape containing rare species of plants and wildlife and with many fragile habitats, which has been established as a nature reserve. Concerns about protecting this environment from the pressures caused by visitors, together with the need to increase employment in the area, have led to plans for local people to get involved with visitors. The aim is to draw on the local knowledge of farmers, fishermen and others in the community, and enable them to develop the ability to act as both guides to and managers of the reserve. There are also plans for the resources of the Lough Adoon Valley Bronze Age site to be identified and assessed, in the hope that this can be made more accessible to the public as a heritage attraction.

There's an increasing emphasis on heritage and culture within tourism, reflected both in the government's new National Development Plan and in the recent policies of the Irish Tourist Board. Heritage attractions are popular in Ireland: in 1993, 6.9 million visits were made to them, and areas with heritage features are being increasingly visited. Yet many of the features which illustrate Ireland's history – castles, great houses, thatched cottages, old mills – are under severe threat, partly because relatively few have survived the troubles of history intact. The Irish Tourist Board's new strategy includes initiatives designed to prevent this element of the country's heritage being lost, by finding new uses for such properties, and establishing a Landmark Trust for Ireland.

In some places those involved in developing cultural tourism – the fastest growing sector within the industry – are also concerned with the preservation and enhancement of the Irish language. This is particularly the case in areas such as Donegal, one of the main Gaelic-speaking regions, and an immensely popular area for tourists. Many community groups and artists are helping to bring about a cultural renaissance and a revival of pride in the Irish language and traditions, at the same time creating jobs in areas badly hit by poverty and unemployment.

One of the most successful projects is at Dunlewey in Donegal, situated at the foot of Mount Errigal. Over the years this farming area has suffered from emigration and migration, with the population falling to just two hundred. Then, in 1986, local people bought a cottage, farm and shop formerly belonging to a famous Donegal weaver, and converted it into a lakeside centre, with a reconstruction and interpretation of a typical life of a weaver in the middle of the nineteenth century. There are other attractions based at the centre, including demonstrations of traditional crafts, opportunities for salmon and trout fishing, a farmyard, a children's play area, and boat trips on Dunlewey Lough. There are also plans for the building of self-catering accommodation.

The centre has breathed fresh life into the area, and now employs twenty-five people. In 1993 it attracted 25,000 visitors, making it the biggest community-owned venture in the county. But perhaps the most unusual element of the project is the language one. All workers at the centre have to be Irish speakers, a feature which has attracted many Irish-speaking holiday-makers to the area. The whole project is bound up with the desire of local people, against the prevailing tide of English, to preserve Irish as a living language; but making it a distinctive feature for tourists also makes commercial sense.

Another Donegal project aimed at preserving traditional culture is the folk village museum at Glencolmcille. It was to the valleys in this region that the first farmers came to Ireland five thousand years ago, and the area is rich in standing stones and other ancient monuments. But the museum concentrates on the way of life in more recent times: it includes replicas of traditional cottages of the last three centuries, equipped with the furniture, artefacts and utensils of the different periods.

Rural tourism, then, is seen as a key component for the future of tourist activity in Ireland. The control of developments by local people, together with the sustainable policies of their main funders, suggest they will remain appropriate in scale, and sensitive to the need to preserve the country's abundant natural riches. The Irish Tourist Board's new strategy accepts that there is a limit to growth, and an optimal number of tourists. 'Optimality' takes into account social costs such as environmental damage, congestion, time losses, inconvenience and disruption of local communities by more tourism.

The way forward, it believes, is to spread business more evenly through the year and around the country, and to concentrate not on increasing the number of visitors, but on meeting the needs of the more independent tourist who is mindful of environmental issues. 'Appreciation of environmental quality has become a major factor in holiday choice in the 1990s,' it states, 'so our environment is truly an asset whose time has come.'

For the future, there are indications of a growing desire on both sides of the Irish border for cooperation between tourist and other bodies, a fact reflected in the setting-up of a number of cross-border initiatives, with European funding support, in the autumn of 1994. A good example is to be found on the 500 miles of the Shannon-Erne Waterway, which has just been reopened to leisure cruises and barges. Here, through a £30 million scheme backed by both Irish and UK governments, the border simply does not exist.

National Park Visitor Centres

Ireland has three well-established national parks, in Glenveagh, Killarney and Connemara. Discussions are also well advanced about creating one in the Nephin Beg area of County Mayo, which may become a reality by the end of the century. But it's the proposals for visitor centres in two of the newest parks, in The Burren and the Wicklow Mountains (as well as for one in a National Historic Park), that have recently stirred up a furious controversy and prompted a national debate on the subject.

The former case is probably the more controversial one. The Burren is a vast limestone area in Counties Clare and Galway, rich in fossils and in plants that rarely grow elsewhere in Ireland. The government, which is responsible for the national parks, announced the establishment of one in The Burren in 1991, to preserve a section of this unique landscape for all time. But its plans to build a visitor centre, intended to maintain a balance between access and conservation, provoked intense criticism amongst conservation groups, the environmental lobby, and some local people – though many of these supported the proposal.

The suggested site for the centre was a disused quarry and reclaimed fields, where it was felt visitors would get a sense of being in the park without having to travel further into it. But critics, while acknowledging the urgent need to manage visitors, argued that it was quite inappropriate for the centre to be positioned in such a remote and wild area, which they felt should not be disturbed in any circumstances. In their view the centre should be located either in a village or, if it had to be in a landscape, then somewhere less wild than the proposed site. The government's argument, which it says is recognised worldwide, is that such centres have to be on-site in order for visitors to be managed in a way that will ensure conservation of the area, and for interpretation to be most effective. It is still awaiting the outcome of its application for planning permission for the centre.

The idea for a visitor centre in the Wicklow Mountains also met with a chorus of disapproval, from local farmers, landowners and conservationists. The national park is in the core area of the uplands region of the mountains, which receives about two million day visitors a year – Dublin is only an hour's journey away. The proposed centre, costing £4 million, is to be located in a particularly scenic area. As in the case of The Burren, opponents argued that the centre should be built in a village rather than in the park itself. After lengthy consultation, the proposal received the go-ahead; but its critics are likely to object to planning permission being given, and to take the matter to appeal.

The disputes over these two centres have stirred up strong emotions on both sides. They have also demonstrated the complexity of the issues involved, and the difficulty of finding the right balance between access, interpretation, and the preservation of unique or fragile landscapes. But the controversy has also resulted in a change in the law. The government can now no longer simply notify a local council of its intentions to build such centres, but has to seek planning permission to do so. This welcome change would seem to strengthen the hands of local people, more of whom are wanting to be involved in decisions about major tourism developments in their localities.

Conclusion: Walking the Talk

'If we really don't try the first step, nothing will change; but perhaps if we make the first step, then everything will change.'

Jost Krippendorf

The projects and initiatives described in this book provide some hope that the principles of sustainable tourism are, however slowly, beginning to be more widely understood. Certainly more people are becoming aware that, unless there are fundamental changes in thinking and behaviour – of governments, of the tourist industry and of tourists themselves – irreparable damage will be done to more and more of the most precious areas of our planet, so that soon few places will be left that are worth visiting.

Yet understanding the seriousness of the situation is of limited value unless it results in action, in 'walking the talk'. What then needs most to be done by the main players in the tourism game in order to preserve the countryside, the coastal areas and the historic sites that we cherish, but which are now in real danger of being 'loved to death'?

Government policies

In some European countries there is continuing and adequate government support for projects and people that are trying to promote sustainable tourism. In the UK, however, to many involved with tourism the government appears not to understand the need to become more directly involved than it is at present. Its insistence that everything can safely be left to the private sector, local government and tourism agencies is seen at best as shortsighted, and at worst as merely cynical – especially since its own task force has acknowledged the need for substantial additional resources.

The government's position is evident in the failure to help sustain the initial momentum of *Maintaining the Balance*, which resulted in a handful of pilot projects being established. The recent drastic cutting of the budget of the English Tourist Board has had a severe effect on the

The new bridge over the river Ehen, linking the Lake District National Park with West Cumbria.

kind of development work that is needed in order to innovate and experiment, and to put into practice the principles of sustainable tourism which that report spelt out. As Tricia Barnett, coordinator of Tourism Concern, puts it: 'The effect is to exclude this kind of development being promoted nationally. Money isn't needed only to resource such initiatives, but to resource people to spread the word. The government is not matching its fine words with the resources that are needed.'[1]

The cutbacks have also affected the regional tourist boards, which are now having to be more concerned with survival than with development. Meanwhile the transfer of tourism from the Department of Employment to the Department of National Heritage appears to have had little positive result. Government support for promoting sustainable tourism remains at best lukewarm.

Some people in the field believe the government should be doing much more in the way of supporting new approaches. Dick Sisman of Green Flag International is one of these: 'The government has bought out most voluntary organisations – apart from Greenpeace – by giving them grants to do what the government wants,' he argues. 'They should be freeing up environmental entrepreneurs so they can act as catalysts, and go in directions that might be uncomfortable or risky for the government, but good for sustainable tourism.'[2]

At present development work is too dependent on the efforts of pioneering individuals at local and regional level. Such people are often in a minority, isolated, and not in key posts. Once they move on or up, such work can be given a lower priority, or even vanish altogether. The work is also hampered by the fact that within local government there is no statutory duty to spend money on tourism: councils will provide leisure services for their own residents, but are generally much more cautious about catering for the needs of visitors.

Scarcity of resources remains a key issue. There is a growing feeling that the government should be reviewing its hands-off policy over tourism. The sticking point appears to be not just political will, but a lack of vision, and a failure on the part of the government to understand or be concerned about how restrictive its policy is proving to those who are working towards sustainable goals for tourism.

The tourist industry

As far as mass tourism is concerned, a major shift in thinking is required on the part of tour operators if real headway is to be made. This is highly problematic, since most companies are driven entirely by commercial considerations. They claim that if they don't follow demand they will go out of business – even though it's clear that demand is becoming much more variable, and that many people's expectations are much higher than they were even ten years ago. Yet if the operators continue to consider their own interests alone, they're likely to end up destroying the very places on which their industry depends. Unfortunately, most still find it easiest to advertise the honeypots.

One or two companies in the UK industry, such as Thomson and British Airways, are beginning to grapple with the issue. In general, sustainable tourism is seen by companies as potentially damaging to their commercial interests, since it could mean restrictions on numbers, on the timing of flights, and on the carrying capacity of the destination. So a crucial question will be how far resorts and other much-visited places are willing or able to exercise control over the way in which they are used, and to put long-term benefits above short-term financial gain.

Some influential voices are suggesting that incentives are needed to encourage the industry to develop sustainable tourism more quickly. The point is made in the report *Loving Them to Death?*, put together by the Federation of Nature and National Parks of Europe: 'These incentives might take the form of grants, higher penalties for damage caused by non-sustainable tourism, and lower taxes for sustainable forms of tourism,' it says. 'In the short term, resources and incentives are needed to speed up the transition from traditional non-sustainable forms of tourism, and to repair the damage that has already been caused.'[3]

Such incentives could, if applied in the UK and Ireland, give encouragement to those running or promoting farm holidays, for which there is clearly a growing demand, which enable visitors to become more sensitive to rural issues, and which provide much-needed income in remote areas.

Another question, both in the UK and elsewhere, will be whether the traditional resorts can regenerate themselves sufficiently and in the right way to halt the decline in their popularity. Concentrating holiday-makers in seaside resorts already built for them is certainly a good way of limiting the damage to more fragile places; but the resorts will still have to improve what they have to offer, in some cases dramatically, to keep in line with people's changing expectations.

In the countryside generally, those involved in accommodating visitors need to consider a range of questions if they are to embrace the notion of sustainable tourism. There are now enough models of good practice, many of them described in this book, to enable businesses large and small to consider how they can provide a better-quality service for their customers, and at the same time help to protect, preserve or improve the local environment. Again a lot comes down to attitude, to the willingness of individuals to consider change, and to look beyond their own interests to those of the wider community.

Much of the innovative work in the UK is being done by people running local area tourism initiatives, or in charge of individual historic sites or buildings. Again their experience – both their successes and their failures – will prove invaluable to others in similar positions, who are now needing to find ways of managing their visitors while protecting the places they come to see.

The tourists

Many of us are now infinitely more aware of the harm we have done and are doing to our planet than we were twenty years ago. Yet when it comes to being tourists, we often tend to switch off our consciences, and carry on as if our activities are having no adverse effect on the environment. Of course leisure is for pleasure, and no one is suggesting it should not be. Many of us prefer crowds to solitude when on holiday. However, it would seem that an increasing number of us are beginning to see the need to think more carefully about the impact our holidays or visits are having on the places we go to. And if values change, so eventually will behaviour.

In the past the tourist industry has defended its practices by claiming to cater for what people want. Whether it has always done so is questionable, since people's choices depend in part on what alternatives are available. The rise in demand for activity, adventure, wildlife and other holidays of this kind suggests that, in the case of a sizeable minority, they have not been catered for in the past. Ultimately, power lies in the hands of the individual tourist. Critical consumers have, for instance, had a significant effect on the buying policies of supermarket chains. Although tourism is a more complex area, if enough people demand certain minimum standards of environmental responsibility within the tourist industry, and shun those businesses and destinations which fail to meet them, then change could come about, however gradually.

Meanwhile we need to face up to the fact that in the very near future we're going to be asked to pay to gain access to places that up to now have been free, or face restrictions as to when we may enter them, in what numbers, and by what means. As tourists, we will also increasingly be asked to contribute to the cost of protecting and maintaining those precious places that hungry generations are relentlessly treading down. This seems a small price to pay to preserve them for our children and for future generations.

Tourism Projects

England

Cumbria Farm Tourism
ADAS Penrith, Agricola House, Gilwilly Trading Estate,
Penrith, Cumbria CA11 9BU
tel: 01768 65651 fax: 01768 899142

Dartmoor Area Tourism Initiative
The Duchy Building, Tavistock Road, Princetown, Devon PL20 6QF
tel: 01822 89567 fax: 01822 89566

Devon and Cornwall Railway Partnership
Faculty of Science, University of Plymouth, Drake Circus,
Plymouth PL4 8AA
tel: 01752 233094 fax: 01752 233095

Eardisley Village Holidays
The Cruck House, Eardisley HR3 6PQ
tel: 01544 327529

Eastbourne Marketing Group
Minster House, York Road, Eastbourne, East Sussex BN21 4ST
tel: 01323 410044 fax: 01323 417541

Lake District Tourism and Conservation Partnership
Brockhole, Windermere, Cumbria LA23 1LJ
tel: 015394 46601 fax: 015394 45555

Lincolnshire Coast Partnership
The Embassy Centre, Grand Parade, Skegness, Lincolnshire PE25 2UN
tel: 01754 761722 fax: 01754 761737

Lizard Peninsula Project
The Yard, Trelowarren, Helston, Cornwall TR12 6AF
tel: 01326 221708 fax: 01326 221788

National Forest
Stanleigh House, Chapel Street, Donisthorpe, Swadlincote,
Derbyshire DE12 7PS
tel: 01530 273816 fax: 01530 273909

Norfolk Coast Project
6 Station Road, Wells-next-the-Sea, Norfolk NR23 1AE
tel: 01328 711533 fax: 01328 711533

North Pennines Tourism Partnership
Barclays Bank Chambers, Front Street, Alston, Cumbria CA9 3SE
tel: 01434 382069 fax: 01434 382653

Peak Tourism Partnership
Eccles House, Eccles Lane, Hope, Derbyshire S30 2RW
tel: 01433 621513 fax: 01433 621776

Project Explore
S.E. Cornwall Discovery Centre, Millpool, Looe, Cornwall PL13 2AF
tel: 01503 263266 fax: 01503 263266

Purbeck Heritage Committee
Purbeck District Council, Westport House, Wareham, Dorset BH20 4PP
tel: 01929 556561 fax: 01929 552688

Settle-Carlisle Railway Development Company
Enterprise Centre, 21 High Street, Gargrave, Skipton,
North Yorkshire BD23 3RP
tel: 01756 749828 fax: 01756 749832

South Devon Green Tourism Initiative
Foxhole, Dartington, Totnes, Devon TQ9 6EB
tel: 01803 864837 fax: 01803 864837

Stratford-upon-Avon Visitor Management Programme
Room 139, Elizabeth House, Church Street, Stratford-upon-Avon,
Warwickshire CV37 6HX
tel: 01789 260109 fax: 01789 260607

Surrey Hills Visitor Project
Leisure and Tourism Unit, Surrey County Council, County Hall,
Kingston-upon-Thames, KT1 2DN
tel: 0181541 9192 fax: 0181541 9871

Tarka Project
Bideford Station, Railway Terrace, East the Water, Bideford EX39 4BB
tel: 01237 424625 fax: 01237 423613

Weston-super-Mare Tourism Development Action Programme
Directorate of Marketing and Development, Woodspring District Council,
Town Hall, Weston-super-Mare, Avon BS23 1UJ
tel: 01934 631701 fax: 01934 612006

Wiltshire Downs Project
Lackham College, Lacock, Chippenham, Wiltshire SN15 2NY
tel: 01249 447930 fax: 01249 447930

Wales

Mid Wales Festival of the Countryside
Frolic Street, Newtown, Powys SY16 1AP
tel: 01686 625384 fax: 01686 629556

South Pembrokeshire Partnership for Action with Rural Communities
The Old School, Station Road, Narberth, Dyfed SA67 8DU
tel: 01834 860965 fax: 01834 8615470

Wye Valley Tourism and Conservation Project
Wye Valley AONB Office, Hadnock Road, Monmouth, Gwent NP5 3NG
tel: 01600 713977 fax: 01600 772051

Scotland

Callanish Centre Project
Western Isles Islands Council, Sandwick Road, Stornoway PA87 2BW
tel: 01851 703773 fax: 01851 705349

Cumnock and Doon Valley Project
Doon Valley Heritage, Dunaskin, Waterside, By Patna, Ayr KA6 7JF
tel: 01292 531144 fax: 01292 531144

EU Life Programme
Highland Regional Council, 2 Achany Road, Dingwall IV15 9JB
tel: 01349 864991 fax: 01349 864675

Kilmartin Glen Project
Department of Planning, Development and Tourism, Argyll and Bute
District Council, Kilmory, Lochgilphead, Argyll PA31 8RT
tel: 01546 602127 fax: 01546 604138

Loch Ness Development Project
Inverness and Nairn Enterprise, Castle Wynd, Inverness IV2 3DW
tel: 01463 713504 fax: 01463 712002

LOCUS Project
The Square, Aberfeldy, Perthshire PH15 2DD
tel: 01887 820956 fax: 01887 820038

Save the Cairngorms Campaign
PO Box 39, Inverness IV1 2RL
tel: 01463 772345 fax: 01463 772345

Skye Footpaths Project
Scottish Natural Heritage, Skye and Lochalsh Sub Office,
Bridge Road, Portree, Isle of Skye IV51 9ER
tel: 01478 613329 fax: 01478 613470

Trossachs Tourism Management Strategy
Burgh Chambers, South Church Street, Callander, Perthshire FK17 8BN
tel: 01877 30309 fax: 01877 31544

Northern Ireland

An Creagan Centre
Mid Ulster Enterprises, Creggan, Omagh, County Tyrone BT79 9AF
tel: 016627 61112 fax: 016627 61116

Fermanagh Tourism Strategic Development Initiative
Fermanagh District Council, Wellington Road, Enniskillen,
County Fermanagh BT74 7EF
tel: 01365 323110 fax: 01365 325511

Lough Neagh Discovery Centre
Oxford Island National Nature Reserve, Oxford Island, Craigavon,
County Armagh BT66 6NJ
tel: 01762 322205 fax: 01762 347438

Mourne Visitor and Environmental Strategy
c/o Mourne Countryside Centre, 91 Central Promenade,
Newcastle, County Down BT33 0HH
tel: 013967 24059 fax: 013967 26493

Navan at Armagh
Killylea Road, Armagh BT60 4LD
tel: 01861 525550 fax: 01861 522323

Peatlands Park
33 Derryhubbert Road, Dungannon BT71 6NW
tel: 01762 851102 fax: 01762 851821

Slieve Gullion Courtyard Project
89 Drumintree Road, Killeavy, Newry, County Down BT35 8SW
tel: 01693 848084 fax: 01693 848028

Ti Chulainn Project
6 Glendesha Road, Mullaghbawn, Newry, County Armagh BT35 9XN
tel: 01693 60668

Republic of Ireland

Ballyhoura Development Ltd
Education Centre, Kilfinane, County Limerick
tel: 00 353 63 91300 fax: 010 353 63 91330

Dunlewey Lakeside Centre
Dunlewey, Letterkenny, County Donegal
tel: 00 353 75 31699 fax: 010 353 75 31699

Glencolmcille Folk Village Museum
Glencolmcille, County Donegal
tel: 00 353 73 30017

Useful Organisations

UK and Ireland: Tourism

Ark
8-10 Bourdon Street, Mayfair,
London W1X 9HX
tel: 0171-439 4567
fax: 0171-409 2663

Association of British Travel Agents
55/57 Newman Street,
London W1P 4AH
tel: 0171-637 2444
fax: 0171-637 0713

Association of Independent Tour
Operators
133a St Margaret's Road,
Twickenham, Middlesex TW1 1RG
tel: 0181-744 3187
fax: 0181-744 3187

British Activity Holiday Association
22 Green Lane, Hersham,
Walton-on-Thames,
Surrey KT12 5HD
tel: 01932 252994
fax: 01932 252994

British Association of Tourist
Officers
c/o Grampian, Highlands and
Aberdeen, St Nicholas House,
Aberdeen AB9 1DE
tel: 01224 522450
fax: 01224 644822

British Incoming Tour Operators
Association
Vigilant House, 120 Wilton Road,
Victoria, London SW1V 1JZ
tel: 0171-931 0601
fax: 0171-828 0531

British Resorts Association
8 Post Office Avenue, Southport
PR9 0US
tel: 0151-934 2286/2288
fax: 0151-934 2287

British Tourist Authority
Thames Tower, Black's Road,
Hammersmith, London W6 9EL
tel: 0181-846 9000
fax: 0181-563 0302

Centre for the Advancement of
Responsive Travel
70 Dry Hill Park Road, Tonbridge,
Kent TN10 3BX
tel: 01732 352757
fax: 0171-704 8224

Countrygoer
67 Grove Road, Ilkley, Yorkshire
LS29 9PQ
tel: 01943 607868
fax: 01943 816745

Country Houses Association
41 Kingsway, London WC2B 6UB
tel: 0171-836 1624
fax: 0171-240 1676

English Tourist Board
Thames Tower, Black's Road,
Hammersmith, London W6 9EL
tel: 0181-846 9000
fax: 0181-563 0302

Farm Holiday Bureau
National Agricultural Centre,
Stoneleigh Park,
Warwickshire CV8 2LZ
tel: 01203 696909
fax: 01203 696630

Green Flag International
l41 High Street, Linton,
Cambridge CB1 6UL
tel: 01223 890250
fax: 01223 890258

Institute of Travel and Tourism
113 Victoria Street, St Albans,
Hertfordshire AL1 3TJ
tel: 01727 54395
fax: 01727 47415

Irish Farm Holidays
2 Michael Street, Limerick
County Limerick
tel: 00 353 61 400 700
fax: 00 353 61 400 771

Irish Tourist Board
Baggot Street Bridge, Dublin 2
tel: 00 353 1 676 5871
fax: 00 353 1 676 47640

Landmark Trust
Shottesbrooke, Maidenhead,
Berkshire SL6 3SW
tel: 01628 825925
fax: 01628 825417

Landmark Trust
27 Rostrevor Road, Rathgar,
Dublin 6
tel: 00 353 1 4970 331
fax: 00 353 1 4965 746

Northern Ireland Tourist Board
St Anne's Court, 59 North Street,
Belfast BT1 1NB
tel: 01232 231221
fax: 01232 240960

Scottish Tourist Board
23 Ravelston Terrace,
Edinburgh EH4 3EU
tel: 0131-332 2433
fax: 0131-343 2023

Tourism Concern
Southlands College, Wimbledon
Parkside, London SW19 5NN
tel: 0181-944 0464
fax: 0181-944 6583

Travel and Tourism Programme
3 Redman Court,
Princes Risborough,
Buckinghamshire HP27 0AA
tel: 01844 344208
fax: 01844 274340

Wales Tourist Board
Brunel House, 2 Fitzalan Road,
Cardiff CF2 1UY
tel: 01222 499909
fax: 01222 485031

UK and Ireland: General

ACRE (Action with Communities in
Rural England)
Somerford Court, Somerford Road,
Cirencester,
Gloucestershire GL7 1TW
tel: 01285 653477
fax: 01285 654537

Ancient Monuments Society
St Ann's Vestry Hall, 2 Church
Entry, London EC4V 5HB
tel: 0171-236 3934
fax: 0171-329 3677

British Trust for Conservation
Volunteers
36 St Mary's, Wallingford,
Oxfordshire OX10 0EU
tel: 0491 839766

Campaign for the Protection of
Rural Wales
Ty Gwyn, 31 High Street,
Welshpool, Powys SY21 7JP
tel: 01938 552525/556212
fax: 01938 552741

Centre for the Study of
Environmental Change
University of Lancaster,
Lancaster LA1 4YF
tel: 01524 65201
fax: 01524 846339

Civic Trust
17 Carlton House Terrace,
London SW1Y 5AW
tel: 0171-930 0914
fax: 0171-321 2181

Common Ground
41 Shelton Street, Covent Garden,
London WC2H 9HJ
tel: 0171-379 3109
fax: 0171-836 5741

Council for Education in World
Citizenship
Seymour Mews House,
Seymour Mews, London W1H 9PE
tel: 0171-935 1752
fax: 0171-935 5548

Council for Environmental
Education
University of Reading,
London Road, Reading RG1 5AQ
tel: 01734 756061
fax: 01734 756264

Council for National Parks
246 Lavender Hill,
London SW11 1LN
tel: 0171-924 4077
fax: 0171-924 5761

Council for the Protection of Rural
England
Warwick House, 25 Buckingham
Palace Road, London SW1W 0PP
tel: 0171-976 6433
fax: 0171-976 6373

Countryside Commission
John Dower House, Crescent Place,
Cheltenham,
Gloucestershire GL50 3RA
tel: 01242 521381
fax: 01242 584270

Countryside Council for Wales
Plas Penrhos, Ffordd Penrhos,
Bangor, Gwynedd LL57 2LQ
tel: 01248 370444
fax: 01248 355782

Countryside Foundation
Bank House, Hebden Bridge, West
Yorkshire HX7 6DL
tel: 01422 845470
fax: 01422 846151

Countryside Recreation Network
Department of City and
Regional Planning, University of
Wales College of Cardiff,
PO Box 906, Cardiff CF1 3YN
tel: 01222 874970
fax: 01222 874970

English Heritage
Fortress House, 23 Savile Row,
London W1X 1AB
tel: 0171-973 3000
fax: 0171-973 3001

English Nature
Northminster House,
Peterborough PE1 1UA
tel: 01733 340345
fax: 01733 68834

Environment Council
21 Elizabeth Street,
London SW1W 9RP
tel: 0171-824 8411
fax: 0171-730 9941

Environmental Transport
Association
The Old Post House, Heath Road,
Weybridge KT13 8RS
tel: 01932 828882
fax: 01932 829015

Field Studies Council
Central Services, Preston Montford
Hall, Montford Bridge,
Shrewsbury SY4 1HW
tel: 01743 850674
fax: 01743 850178

Forestry Commission
Department of Forestry,
231 Corstophine Road,
Edinburgh EH12 7AT
tel: 0131-334 0303
fax: 0131-334 4473

Forestry Trust
The Old Estate Office, Englefield
Road, Theale, Reading,
Berkshire RG7 5DZ
tel: 01734 323 523
fax: 01734 303 130

Friends of the Earth
26-28 Underwood Street,
London N1 7JQ
tel: 0171-490 1555
fax: 0171-490 0881

Gaia Foundation
18 Well Walk, Hampstead,
London NW3 1LD
tel: 0171-453 5000
fax: 0171-431 0551

Greenpeace
Canonbury Villas, London N1 2PN
tel: 0171-354 5100/359 7396
fax: 0171-359 4372/359 4062

Heritage Coast Forum
Manchester Metropolitan
University, St Augustine's,
Lower Chatham Street,
Manchester M15 6BY
tel: 0161-247 1067
fax: 0161-236 7383

Heritage Education Trust
University College of Ripon and
York St John, College Road,
Ripon HG4 2QX
tel: 01969 650294
fax 01969 650294

Historic Scotland
20 Brandon Street,
Edinburgh EH3 5RA
tel: 0131-244 3107
fax: 0131-244 3030

Institute of Leisure and Amenity
Management
Lower Basildon, Reading,
Berkshire RG8 9NE
tel: 01491 874222
fax: 01491 874059

Joint Nature Conservation
Committee
Monkstone House, City Road,
Peterborough PE1 1JY
tel: 01733 62626
fax: 01733 555948

Landlife
The Old Police Station, Lark Lane,
Liverpool L17 8UU
tel: 0151-728 7011
fax: 0151-728 8413

Marine Conservation Society
9 Gloucester Road, Ross-on-Wye,
Herefordshire HR9 5BU
tel: 01989 66017
fax: 01989 67815

National Society for Clean Air and
Environmental Protection
136 North Street,
Brighton BN1 1RG
tel: 01273 326313
fax: 01273 735802

National Trust
36 Queen Anne's Gate,
London SW1H 9AS
tel: 0171-222 9251
fax: 0171-222 5097

Open Spaces Society
25 Bell Street, Henley-on-Thames,
Oxfordshire RG9 2BA
tel: 01491 573535
fax: 01491 573051

Ramblers Association
1/5 Wandsworth Road,
London SW8 2XX
tel: 0171-582 6878
fax: 0171-587 3799

Royal Geographical Society
Kensington Gore,
London SW7 2AR
tel: 0171-589 5466
fax: 0171-584 4447

Royal Society for Nature
Conservation
The Green, Witham Park,
Waterside South, Lincoln LN5 7JR
tel: 01522 544400
fax: 01522 511616

Royal Society for the Protection of
Birds
The Lodge, Sandy,
Bedfordshire SG19 2DL
tel: 01767 680551
fax: 01767 692365

Rural Development Commission
141 Castle Street, Salisbury,
Wiltshire SP1 3TP
tel: 01722 336255
fax: 01722 332769

Rural Development Council for
Northern Ireland
Loughry College, Cookstown,
Belfast BT80 9AA
tel: 016487 66980
fax: 016487 66922

Save Britain's Heritage
68 Battersea High Street,
London SW11 3HX
tel: 0171-228 3336
fax: 0171-223 2714

Scottish Conservation Projects
Trust
Balallan House, 24 Allan Park,
Stirling FK8 2QG
tel: 01786 479697
fax: 01786 465359

Scottish Natural Heritage
Battleby, Redgorton,
Perth PH1 3EW
tel: 01738 27921
fax: 01738 30583/441897

Scottish Environmental Education
Council
University of Stirling,
Stirling FK9 4LA
tel: 01786 467867
fax: 01786 467864

Scottish Field Studies Association
Enochdhu,
Blairgowrie PH10 7PG
tel: 01250 881286
fax: 01250 8814330

Scottish Wildlife and Countryside
Link
PO Box 604, Perth PH2 0TF
tel: 01738 30804
fax: 01738 43290

Society for the Protection of
Ancient Buildings
37 Spital Square, London E1 6DY
tel: 0171-377 1644
fax: 0171-247 5296

Sustainability
The People's Hall,
91-97 Freston Road,
London W11 4BD
tel: 0171-243 1277
fax: 0171-243 0364

Sustainable Agriculture, Food and
Environment Alliance (SAFE)
21 Tower Street,
London WC2H 9NS
tel: 0171-240 1811
fax: 0171-240 1899

Sustrans (Railway Path and Cycle
Route Construction)
35 King Street, Bristol BS1 4DZ
tel: 01272 268893
fax: 01272 294173

Tidy Britain Group
The Pier, Wigan WN3 4EX
tel: 01942 824620
fax: 01942 824778

Transport 2000
Walkden House, 10 Melton Street,
London NW1 2EJ
tel: 0171-388 8386
fax: 0171-388 2481

United Nations Environment and
Development UK Committee
3 Whitehall Court,
London SW1A 2EL
tel: 0171-930 8169
fax: 0171-930 5893

Wildfowl and Wetlands Trust
Slimbridge, Gloucester GL2 7BT
tel: 01453 890333
fax: 01453 890827

Women's Environmental Network
Trust
Aberdeen Studios, 22 Highbury
Grove, London N5 2EA
tel: 0171-354 8823
fax: 0171-354 0464

Worldaware (Centre for World
Development Education)
1 Catton Street,
London WC1R 4AB
tel: 0171-831 3844
fax: 0171-831 1746

World Wide Fund for Nature UK
Panda House, Weyside Park,
Catteshall Lane, Godalming,
Surrey GU7 1XR
tel: 01483 426444
fax: 01483 426409

Youth Hostels Association
Trevelyan House, 8 St Stephen's
Hill, St Albans,
Hertfordshire AL1 2DY
tel: 01727 855215
fax: 01727 844126

European and International: Tourism

Coalition on Child Prostitution and
Tourism
c/o Anti-Slavery International, Unit
4, Stableyard, Broomgrove Road,
London SW9 9TL
tel: 0171-924 9555
fax: 0171-738 4110

Ecumenical Coalition on Third
World Tourism
PO Box 35, Senanikhom PO,
Bangkok 10902, Thailand
tel: 00 662 939 7111
fax: 00 662 939 7112

European Tour Operators
Association
26-28 Paradise Road, Richmond,
Surrey TW9 1SE
tel: 0181-332 0014
fax: 0181-784 2808

World Tourism Organisation
Capitan Haya 42, 28020 Madrid,
Spain
tel: 00 341 571 0628
fax: 00 341 571 3733

World Travel and Tourism Council
Suffolk Place, Haymarket,
London SW1Y 4BS
tel: 0171-222 1955
fax: 0171-222 4983

European and International: General

Alp Action
20 Quai Gustave-ador
1207 Geneva
Switzerland
tel: 00 41 22 736 8181
fax: 00 41 22 736 8060

Earthwatch Europe
Belsyre Court, 57 Woodstock
Road, Oxford OX2 6HU
tel: 01865 311600
fax: 01865 311383

Europa Nostra
Lange Voorhut 35, 2514 EC, The
Hague, Netherlands
tel: 00 317 035 17865

Europe Conservation
Via Fusetti 14, 20143 Milano, Italy
tel: 00 392 5810 3135
fax: 00 392 8940 0649

European Blue Flag
Lion House, Muspole Street,
Norwich NR3 1DJ
tel: 01603 762888
fax: 01603 760580

Federation of Nature and National
Parks of Europe
Kröllstrasse 5, D-8352 Grafenau,
Germany
tel: 00 49 8552 2839
fax: 00 49 8552 3242

International Institute for
Environment and Development
3 Endsleigh Street,
London WC1H 0DD
tel: 0171-388 2117
fax: 0171-388 2826

Survival International
310 Edgware Road,
London W2 1DY
tel: 0171-723 5535
fax: 0171-723 4059

World Conservation Union
Avenue de Mont Blanc,
CH-1196 Gland, Switzerland
tel: 00 41 22 649 114
fax: 00 41 22 642 926

Notes

Full details of publications referred to in the notes can be found in the section on Further Reading.

1 The Scale of the Problem
1 'Boycott paradise', *In Focus*, summer 1994, page 10.
2 *Loving Them to Death?*, page 43.
3 'Finding the right track', David Nicholson-Lord, *The Independent on Sunday*, 3 October 1993; *Beyond the Green Horizon*, pages 37-39; 'The economics of ecotourism', Paul Steele, *In Focus*, autumn 1993, page 4.
4 *Loving Them to Death?*, page 49.

2 Sustainable Tourism
1 *Loving Them to Death?*, page 5.
2 Letter to author.

3 Country Matters
1 Dartmoor Area Tourism Initiative, 1994 report.
2 'Meeting rural housing needs', Action with Communities in Rural England, 1994.
3 Speech at conference 'Leisure: The New Dilemma', London, 12 May 1994.
4 *Leisure Landscapes*, pages 14-15.
5 'Local Plan', North York Moors National Park, 1992, page 54.

4 Obstacles to Change
1 *Challenges and Choices for the 90s*, page 11.
2 Interview with author.
3 Interview with author.
4 Interview with author.
5 *Challenges and Choices for the 90s*, page 59.
6 Interview with author.
7 Interview with author.
8 *Challenges and Choices for the 90s*, page 53.
9 'Restoring the balance', *In Focus*, spring 1992, page 12.
10 'Tourism and the environment: English task force steams to the rescue', paper for Rural Tourism Unit, University of Bristol, June 1991, page 3.

11 Interview with author.

12 Interview with author.

13 Speech to conference on 'Tourism, Economic Regeneration and Employment', London, 28 October 1994.

14 Letter to author, 15 March 1994.

15 Interview with author.

16 Interview with author.

5 Limiting the Damage

1   Interview with author.

2   *The Green Light,* page 30.

3   'Interpretation and sustainable tourism: the potential and the pitfalls', *Journal of Sustainable Tourism*, vol. 1, no. 2, 1993, page 71.

4   *Maintaining the Balance*, page 23.

5   Interview with Roy Minter by author.

6   *Challenges and Choices for the 90s*, page 34.

7   Letter to author.

8   'Submission to the English Tourist Board for core funding', May 1991, page 5.

6 Getting There

1   Speech at conference 'Leisure: The New Dilemma', London 12 May 1994.

7 Business Matters

1   Interview with author.

2   *Holidays That Don't Cost the Earth*, page 300.

3   *Challenges and Choices for the 90s*, page 65.

4   Interview with author.

5   *The Green Light*, page 5.

6   'First year report,' South Devon Green Tourism Initiative, December 1993, page 8.

7   'Green tourism action', *Heritage Coast*, September 1992, page 4.

8 Acting Locally

1 'Sustainable rural tourism strategies: a tool for development and conservation', *Journal of Sustainable Tourism*, vol. 2, nos 1 & 2, 1994, page 102.
2 Interview with author.
3 Interview with author.
4 Letter to author.
5 Richard Denman, 'The market for rural community tourism,' *Rural Community Tourism*, page 11.
6 John Myerscough, *The Economic Importance of the Arts*.
7 'Communicating the message', *Scotland's Natural Heritage*, no.3, April 1994, page 11.

Conclusion: Walking the Talk

1 Interview with author.
2 Interview with author.
3 *Loving Them to Death?*, page 60.

Boxed Information

(Numerals refer to page numbers.)

8 'A European strategy for the Alps?', *Alp Action*, 1993.
13 Geoffrey Wall, 'International collaboration in the search for sustainable tourism in Bali', *Journal of Sustainable Tourism*, vol. 1, no. 1, 1993, page 38.
25 Letter to author, 19 May 1994.
28 Victoria Brittain, 'The canny key to paradise', *Guardian*, 10 September 1993.
44 Ed Vulliamy, 'Disney's invading host forces re-run of Civil War battle', *Observer*, 19 June 1994.
46 David Cohen, 'Lost in the rough', *Guardian*, 24 September 1994.
61 John Vidal, 'A slow death in paradise', *Guardian*, 22 April 1994.
64 Anna Borzello, 'Campaign News', *In Focus*, summer 1992, page 17.
79 Letter to author, 20 July 1994.
82 'The Himalayan Tourist Code', Tourism Concern, London, 1991.
97 *Loving Them to Death?*, page 38.

100 *Tourism in National Parks*, page 19.
114 'Bekal zoned for tourism urbanisation', *In Focus*, summer 1994.
119 Paul Webster, 'Bretons bulldoze back to nature', *Guardian*, 22 February 1994.
137 *Beyond the Green Horizon*, page 40.
140 Reverend Kaleo Patterson, 'Aloha for sale', *In Focus*, summer 1992, page 4.

Further Reading

Books

DEROUNIAN, James Garo, *Another Country: Real Life Beyond Rose Cottage*, NCVO Publications, 1993.

ELKINGTON, John, and HAILES, Julia, *Holidays That Don't Cost the Earth*, Victor Gollancz, 1992.

HEWISON, Robert, *The Heritage Industry: Britain in a Climate of Decline*, Methuen, 1987.

JAMES, Henry, *English Hours*, Oxford University Press, 1981.

LEWIS, Norman, *Voices of the Old Sea*, Hamish Hamilton, 1984.

LODGE, David, *Paradise News*, Secker & Warburg, 1991.

MABEY, Richard, *The Common Ground*, 2nd edition, Dent, 1993.

MYERSCOUGH, John, *The Economic Importance of the Arts in Britain*, Policy Studies Institute, 1988.

PRIESTLEY, J.B., *English Journey*, Penguin, 1977.

SINCLAIR, David, *Shades of Green: Myth and Muddle in the Countryside*, Grafton, 1990.

TILDEN, Freeman, *Interpreting Our Heritage*, University of North Carolina Press, 1957.

WOOD, Katie, and HOUSE, Syd, *The Good Tourist: A Worldwide Guide for the Green Traveller*, Mandarin, 1991.

WRIGHT, Patrick, *On Living in an Old Country*, Verso, 1985.

Reports

Association of County Councils, *Promoting Tourism*, 1993.

Council for the Protection of Rural England, *Leisure Landscapes: Leisure, Culture and the English Countryside: Challenges and Conflicts*, 1994.

Countryside Commission, *Planning for a Greener Countryside*, 1989.

Countryside Commission, *Fit for the Future: Report of the National Parks Review Panel*, 1991.

Department of the Environment, *Sustainable Development: The UK Strategy*, Her Majesty's Stationery Office, 1994.

English Tourist Board/Department of Employment, *Maintaining the Balance: Tourism and the Environment*, 1991.

English Tourist Board, *Tourism in National Parks: A Guide to Good Practice*, 1991.

English Tourist Board, *The Green Light: A Guide to Sustainable Tourism*, 1992.

English Tourist Board/Civic Trust, *Turning the Tide: A Heritage and Environment Strategy for a Seaside Resort*, 1993.

Federation of Nature and National Parks, *Loving Them to Death? Sustainable Tourism in Europe's Nature and National Parks*, 1993.

LANDRY, Charles, MONTGOMERY, John, and WORPOLE, Ken, *The Last Resort: Tourism, Tourist Employment and 'PostTourism' in the South East,* Comedia, 1989.

Museums and Galleries Commission, *Museums and Tourism: Mutual Benefit*, 1993.

Tourism Concern/World Wide Fund for Nature, *Beyond the Green Horizon: Principles for Sustainable Tourism*, 1992.

United Nations Commission on Environment and Development, *Our Common Future,* Oxford University Press, 1987.

Conference Proceedings

English Tourist Board/Department of National Heritage, *Tourism and the Environment: Challenges and Choices for the 90s*, 1993.

Heritage Coast Forum, *Coastal Heritage '93*, 1993.

Northern Ireland Tourist Board, *Rural Community Tourism*, 1994.

University of Ljubljana, *Educating for Sustainable Tourism*, 1992.

Magazines and Journals

Annals of Tourism Research, Pergamon Press.

Countrygoer News, Transport for Leisure.

Countryside, Countryside Commission.

Countryside Campaigner, Council for the Protection of Rural England.

Earth Matters, Friends of the Earth.

In Focus, Tourism Concern.

Journal of Sustainable Tourism, Channel View Publications.

The Magazine, National Trust.

National Parks Today, Countryside Commission/ Countryside Council for Wales.

Rural Focus, Rural Development Commission.

Scotland's Natural Heritage, Scottish Natural Heritage.

Index